HomeBuild

Guiding Your
Teenagers

By Dennis and Barbara Rainey

*"Unless the Lord
builds the house,
its builders
labor in vain"*
(Psalm 127:1a).

FAMILYLIFE
Bringing Timeless Principles Home
Little Rock, Arkansas

Group
Loveland, Colorado

Group's R.E.A.L. Guarantee to you:

This Group resource incorporates our R.E.A.L. approach to ministry—one that encourages long-term retention and life transformation. It's ministry that's:

Relational
Because learner-to-learner interaction enhances learning and builds Christian friendships.

Experiential
Because what learners experience through discussion and action sticks with them up to 9 times longer than what they simply hear or read.

Applicable
Because the aim of Christian education is to equip learners to be both hearers and doers of God's Word.

Learner-based
Because learners understand and retain more when the learning process takes into consideration how they learn best.

Credits
FamilyLife
Editor: David Boehi

Group Publishing, Inc.
Editor: Matt Lockhart
Chief Creative Officer: Joani Schultz
Copy Editor: Dena Twinem
Art Directors: Jenette L. McEntire and Jean Bruns
Print Production Artist: Nancy Serbus
Cover Art Director: Jeff A. Storm
Cover Designer: Alan Furst, Inc.
Cover Photographer: Daniel Treat
Illustrator: Ken Jacobson
Production Manager: Peggy Naylor

ISBN 0-7644-2546-3
10 9 8 7 6 5 4 3 2 1   12 11 10 09 08 07 06 05 04 03

Printed in the United States of America.

How to Let the Lord Build Your House
and not labor in vain

The HomeBuilders Parenting Series™: A small-group
Bible study dedicated to making your family all that God
intended.

FamilyLife is a division of Campus Crusade for Christ
International, an evangelical Christian organization founded in
1951 by Bill Bright. FamilyLife was started in 1976 to help fulfill
the Great Commission by strengthening marriages and families
and then equipping them to go to the world with the gospel of
Jesus Christ. The Weekend to Remember conference is held in
most major cities throughout the United States and is one of the
fastest-growing marriage conferences in America today.
"FamilyLife Today," a daily radio program hosted by Dennis
Rainey, is heard on hundreds of stations across the country.
Information on all resources offered by FamilyLife may be
obtained by contacting us at the address, telephone number, or
World Wide Web site listed below.

Dennis Rainey, Executive Director
FamilyLife
P.O. Box 8220
Little Rock, AR 72221-8220
1-800-FL-TODAY
www.familylife.com

A division of Campus Crusade for Christ International
Bill Bright, Founder
Steve Douglass, President

About the Sessions

Each session in this study is composed of the following categories: Warm-Up, Blueprints, Wrap-Up, and HomeBuilders Project. A description of each of these categories follows:

Warm-Up (15 minutes)

 The purpose of Warm-Up is to help people unwind from a busy day and get to know each other better. Typically the first point in Warm-Up is an exercise that is meant to be fun while introducing the topic of the session. The ability to share in fun with others is important in building relationships. Another component of Warm-Up is the Project Report (except in Session One), which is designed to provide accountability for the HomeBuilders Project that is to be completed by couples between sessions.

Blueprints (60 minutes)

This is the heart of the study. In this part of each session, people answer questions related to the topic of study and look to God's Word for understanding. Some of the questions are to be answered by couples, in subgroups, or in the group at large. There are notes in the margin or instructions within a question that designate these groupings.

Wrap-Up (15 minutes)

This category serves to "bring home the point" and wind down a session in an appropriate fashion.

HomeBuilders Project (60 minutes)

This project is the unique application step in a HomeBuilders study. Before leaving each meeting, couples are encouraged to "Make a Date" to complete the project for the session prior to the next group meeting. Most HomeBuilders Projects contain three sections: (1) As a Couple—a brief exercise designed to get the date started; (2) Individually—a section of questions for husbands and wives to answer separately; and (3) Interact as a Couple—an opportunity for couples to share their answers with each other and to make application in their lives.

Another feature you will find in this course is a section of Parent-Teen Interactions. There is a corresponding interaction for each session. These interactions provide parents an excellent opportunity to communicate with their children on the important topics covered in this course.

In addition to the above regular features, occasional activities are labeled "For Extra Impact." These are activities that generally provide a more active or visual way to make a particular point. Be mindful that people within a group have different learning styles. While most of what is presented is verbal, a visual or active exercise now and then helps engage more of the senses and appeals to people who learn best by seeing, touching, and doing.

About the Authors

Dennis Rainey is the executive director and the co-founder of FamilyLife (a division of Campus Crusade for Christ) and a graduate of Dallas Theological Seminary. Since 1976, he has overseen the rapid growth of FamilyLife's conferences and resources. He began the HomeBuilders Couples Series and the HomeBuilders Parenting Series and is also the daily host of the nationally syndicated radio program "FamilyLife Today."

Dennis and his wife, Barbara, have spoken at FamilyLife conferences across the United States and overseas. Dennis is also a speaker for Promise Keepers. He has testified on family issues before Congress and has appeared on numerous radio and television programs.

Dennis and Barbara have co-authored several books, including *Building Your Mate's Self-Esteem* (re-released as *The New Building Your Mate's Self-Esteem*), *Moments Together for Couples*, *Parenting Today's Adolescent*, and *Starting Your Marriage Right*.

Dennis and Barbara have served on the staff of Campus Crusade since 1971. They have six children and a growing number of grandchildren. They are both graduates of the University of Arkansas and live near Little Rock, Arkansas.

Contents

Acknowledgments **8**

Introduction **9**

Session One: The Traps of Adolescence **13**

Session Two: Peer Pressure.......................................**31**

Session Three: Sex **45**

Session Four: Dating...**59**

Session Five: Media..**75**

Session Six: Substance Abuse **89**

Parent-Teen Interactions..**104**

Where Do You Go From Here?..**117**

Our Problems, God's Answers **120**

Leaders Notes...**130**

Acknowledgments

As we write these words, our youngest child is nearing the end of her senior year of high school, and we are wrapping up our years of guiding six children through the traps of adolescence. It is appropriate that we thank our children—Ashley, Benjamin, Samuel, Rebecca, Deborah, and Laura—for putting up with imperfect parents who have attempted to apply biblical principles to the art of parenting. We have no greater joy than to know that our children are walking in the truth (3 John 4).

There are great men and women who I work with here at FamilyLife. One of them is Dave Boehi—he is not only a gifted writer, but also a man with a huge heart for the world. Dave, you have been The Man when it comes to creating HomeBuilders studies. Your life has touched hundreds of thousands of lives around the world. This series would never have happened without you.

Ken Tuttle is another unsung hero in the battle for the family. Ken, you have been instrumental in taking these studies and moving them from the bookshelf to the hearts of homes around the world. Thanks for your faithful leadership.

Mike Pickle was a great help in putting this study together. And to the team that keeps me going—Clark Hollingsworth, Janet Logan, Michele English, and John Majors—thanks for the lives you have served and that are forever changed because you cared. Thanks for your faithfulness and hard work!

A special word of thanks to Matt Lockhart, our editor at Group Publishing, for his continued partnership over the last few years with both the HomeBuilders Couples Series and the HomeBuilders Parenting Series. Matt has led many of the studies himself and provides a high level of expertise in helping us craft these studies.

Finally, this study is dedicated—along with our companion book, *Parenting Today's Adolescent*, to the hundreds of students we taught in our sixth-grade Sunday school classes at Fellowship Bible Church. Thanks for letting us have so much fun as we helped you prepare for adolescence.

Introduction

Nearly all of the important jobs in our culture require intensive training. We would not think of allowing someone to practice medicine, for example, without first attending medical school and completing his or her residency.

But do you realize that most people receive little training to fulfill one of the most important responsibilities of our lives—how to be effective parents? When we bring a new life into the world, we burst with pride and joy...but are often ignorant of how to actually raise that child to become a mature, responsible adult.

In response to the need we see in families today, FamilyLife and Group Publishing have developed a series of small-group studies called the HomeBuilders Parenting Series. These studies focus on raising children and are written so that parents of children of all ages, from the cradle until they leave home, will benefit.

For these HomeBuilders studies, we have several goals in mind: First, *we want to encourage you in the process of child rearing.* We feel that being a mom and a dad is a high calling and an incredible privilege. We also know how easy it is to feel overwhelmed by the responsibility, especially when you have young children. Participating in a HomeBuilders group can connect you with other parents who share your struggles. The help and encouragement you receive from them will be invaluable.

Second, *we want to help you develop a practical, biblical plan for parenting.* It's so easy as parents to take parenting one day at a time. But as we've raised our six children, we've learned that we need to understand biblical guidelines on parenting and then make proactive plans on how we will apply them.

Third, *we want to enhance and strengthen your teamwork as a couple.* You will learn together how to apply key biblical truths, and in the HomeBuilders Projects, you will talk through how to apply them to your unique family situation. In the process, you will have the opportunity to discuss issues that you may have ignored or avoided in the past. And you'll spend time regularly in prayer, asking God for his direction and power.

Fourth, *we want to help you connect with other parents so you can encourage and help each other.* You could complete this study alone with your spouse, but we strongly urge you to either form or join a group of couples studying this material. You will find that the questions in each study will help create a special environment of warmth, encouragement, and fellowship as you meet together to study how to build the type of home you desire. You will have the opportunity to talk with other parents to learn some new ideas...or to get their advice...or just to see that others are going through the same experiences. Participating in a HomeBuilders group could be one of the highlights of your life.

Finally, *we want to help you strengthen your relationship with God.* Our loving Father not only provides biblical principles for parenting, but through our relationship with him, we also can rely on his strength and wisdom. In fact, it is when we feel most powerless and inadequate as a parent that he is most real to us. God loves to help the helpless parent.

The Bible: Blueprints for Building Your Family

You will notice as you proceed through this study that the Bible is used frequently as the final authority on issues of life, marriage, and parenting. Although written thousands of years ago, this Book still speaks clearly and powerfully about the struggles we face in our families. The Bible is God's Word—his blueprints for building a God-honoring home and for dealing with the practical issues of living.

We encourage you to have a Bible with you for each session. For this series we use the New International Version as our primary reference. Another excellent translation is the New American Standard Bible.

A Special Word to Single Parents

Although the primary audience for this study is married couples, we also recognize that single parents will benefit greatly from the experience. If you are a single parent, you will find that some of the language and material does not apply directly to you. But most of what you will find in this study is timeless wisdom taken directly from Scripture that can help you develop a solid, workable plan for your family. We hope you will be flexible and adapt the material to your specific situation. If possible, you might want to attend the group sessions with another single parent. This will allow you to encourage each other and hold each other accountable to complete the HomeBuilders Projects.

Ground Rules

Each group is designed to be enjoyable and informative—and non-threatening. Three simple ground rules will help ensure that everyone feels comfortable and gets the most out of the experience.

1. Don't share anything that would embarrass your spouse or violate the trust of your children.

2. You may pass on any question you don't want to answer.

3. If possible, plan to complete the HomeBuilders Project as a couple between group sessions.

A Few Quick Notes About Leading a HomeBuilders Group

1. Leading a group is much easier than you may think! A group leader in a HomeBuilders session is really a "facilitator." As a facilitator, your goal is simply to guide the group through the discussion questions. You don't need to teach the material—in fact, we don't want you to! The special dynamic of a HomeBuilders group is that couples teach themselves.

2. This material is designed to be used in a home study, but it also can be adapted for use in a Sunday school environment. (See page 131 for more information about this option.)

3. We have included a section of Leaders Notes in the back of this book. Be sure to read through these notes before leading a session; they will help you prepare.

4. For more material on leading a HomeBuilders group, get a copy of the *HomeBuilders Leader Guide*, by Drew and Kit Coons. This book is an excellent resource that provides helpful guidelines on how to start a study, how to keep discussion moving, and much more.

Recommended Reading

We originally developed the concepts in this study for a book titled *Parenting Today's Adolescent*. You will find this book to be an invaluable companion as you develop a plan for talking to your children about the traps of adolescence.

The Traps of Adolescence

To pass biblical convictions to your teenage children that will equip them to avoid the traps of adolescence, you need to stay connected with them.

W A R M • U P   15 M I N U T E S

Growing Up Is Hard to Do

Introduce yourself, and tell the group the names and ages of your children. Then answer one or two of the following questions:

- Think back to the years when you began to move from childhood into the teenage years. What were some of the ways you began to change as you went through those years?
- As a sixteen year old, what do you remember as being one of your biggest priorities or problems?
- What is one way your teenager reminds you of yourself at that age?

- What is one thing you hope to gain from this study?

Getting Connected

Pass your books around the room, and have everyone write in their names, phone numbers, and e-mail addresses.

_____

NAME, PHONE, AND E-MAIL

_____

NAME, PHONE, AND E-MAIL

_____

NAME, PHONE, AND E-MAIL

_____

NAME, PHONE, AND E-MAIL

_____

NAME, PHONE, AND E-MAIL

_____

NAME, PHONE, AND E-MAIL

BLUEPRINTS   60 MINUTES

Read aloud the case study, with volunteer readers for each of the three parts.

Case Study

Mike and Lori are having a conversation about their daughter, Lauren.

Mike: I guess Lauren is growing up faster than I want.

Lori: What do you mean?

Mike: She doesn't seem to want to do anything with me any- more. I just asked if she wanted to go get some doughnuts— like we have every Saturday morning ever since she was two years old. Now she doesn't seem to care about it.

Lori: I know what you mean. She used to run up and hug me whenever she saw me at her school. Now she acts like she's embarrassed to see me.

Mike: I guess I knew this was coming, but I didn't realize it would start when she was twelve. She's not even a teenager yet.

Lauren enters the room.

Lauren: I'm going to the mall this afternoon with Alyssa.

Lori: Really? I don't remember any discussion about us going to the mall.

Lauren: It's just the mall, Mom. I didn't realize I had to ask permission for everything I do.

Lori: And how were you planning to get there, young lady?

Lauren: Alyssa's brother is going to take us, and we were going to have you pick us up.

Lori: Thanks for asking.

Mike: Hold on a minute. I'm not so sure I like the idea of you two going to the mall without a parent. I'm not sure it's safe for girls your age.

Lauren: But, Dad, all our friends do it. We're going to meet them there.

Mike: Let me talk to your mother about it, and we'll decide.

Lauren: Why are you always so strict? None of the other kids' parents seem to have a problem with this.

Mike: Your mother and I will discuss it, and we'll get back to you.

Lauren: Well, hurry up. I've got to call Alyssa to let her know.

Lauren exits in a cloud of dissatisfaction.

Lori: Is this how I acted with my parents when I was that age?

If you have a large group, form smaller groups of about six people to answer the Blueprints questions. Unless otherwise noted, answer the questions in your subgroup. Before moving into the Wrap-Up section, have sub-groups report to the whole group the highlights from their discussion.

1. How can you relate to the situation Mike and Lori face with their daughter? In what ways has your child been showing a greater desire for independence?

2. What advice would you give Mike and Lori?

Drifting Apart

We like to call the time period before children enter adolescence the "golden years." These are the years (ages six to eleven) when parenting seems easier for many. Your children actually listen to you and enjoy your company. Then, as they approach and enter adolescence, their growing need for independence often leads them to think they no longer need much input from parents or other adults. Instead, they rely on their peers. Popular media and advertising often encourage this type of thinking, portraying parents as being old-fashioned and restrictive while teenagers are shown as being capable of making wise decisions.

Another thing often happens when children turn twelve or thirteen: Not only do they begin pushing their parents away, but their parents also begin pulling away from them. Research has shown that a surprising number of parents become less involved with their children as they go through adolescence.

3. What is your opinion of the idea that teenagers require less guidance from parents?

4. Read Proverbs 22:15. What do you think this verse means when it says "Foolishness is bound up in the heart of a child" (New American Standard Bible)? What are ways and reasons teenagers demonstrate foolishness at times?

5. Why do you think the level of parent-child involvement often decreases during adolescence? Take a minute to write down some reasons why you think this happens. Then share one or two of your thoughts with the group.

Reasons children begin spending less time at home as they go through adolescence:	*Reasons parents begin reducing their involvement with their teenage children:*

Keeping the Connection

As God was creating the nation of Israel, the family was established as one of the key foundations for the society. Parents were given responsibility to tell their children about God, to teach each succeeding generation about the Bible.

6. Read through the instructions given to parents in Deuteronomy 6:1-9. What does this passage say about

- the personal character that should be found in parents?

- the type of relationship parents should have with their children in order to teach them about God and the Bible?

HomeBuilders Principle:
To help your children grow up to walk with God, you need to take the initiative to remain involved during the adolescent years.

Recognizing the Traps

During their teenage years, children face a lot of different pressures and problems that we like to call the traps of adolescence. These are the snares that entice and lure a teenager into making foolish choices. Many of us were caught by some of these traps ourselves when we were teenagers.

For example, one obvious trap is sex. We live in a culture that encourages young people to experiment with sex at a very early age.

7. What are some other traps you can think of?

8. What is one thing your parents did that helped prepare you for the traps you faced as a teen? What is one thing you wish they had done?

Walking in the Truth

One of the reasons why teenagers are so easily caught in the traps of adolescence is that many have only a vague set of beliefs to guide their behavior and their choices. Even teens who call themselves Christians often don't know what they believe, and don't understand how the truth of the Bible can influence their daily lives.

9. Read 3 John 3-4. What do you think it means for children to be "walking in the truth," and why is this important in our culture today? How does walking in the truth differ from walking in lies?

10. Practically, what are some things you can do as a parent to provide biblical and spiritual instruction to your children?

A Legacy of Biblical Convictions

One of the keys for helping teenagers learn to walk in the truth is for you to pass on biblical convictions that will help them make good choices. What is a conviction? We like the definition author Josh McDowell presents in his book *Beyond Belief to Convictions*.

Having a conviction, he writes, "is being so thoroughly convinced that something is absolutely true that you take a stand for it regardless of the consequences."

That is what your children need—a set of biblical convictions that will help them negotiate the traps of adolescence. One reason many parents do not pass on biblical convictions to their children is they haven't clarified their own convictions.

Answer questions 11 and 12 with your spouse. After answering, you may want to share an appropriate insight or discovery with the group.

11. Individually, take a minute to look over the following list of various traps of adolescence. Select one of these for which you have particularly strong convictions. Then write a sentence that expresses one of your convictions and share it with your spouse.

Peer pressure: the influence peers have in one's life
For example: Bad company corrupts good character.

Sex: biblical standards for purity before marriage

Dating: guidelines for spending time with the opposite sex

Media: standards on what to watch, read, or listen to and on how much time to devote to media

Appearance: appropriate dress and grooming for different occasions

Attitude: maintaining a proper perspective on yourself, your parents, and authority figures

Substance abuse: using alcohol, drugs, and other potentially harmful substances

Pornography: exposing yourself to images that degrade God's standards on sex

12. Why is it important for your children to know your convictions and to see you model them?

HomeBuilders Principle:
Now is the time to clarify and begin modeling your biblical convictions on real-life issues your teenager will face.

After completing the Wrap-Up activity, close this session in prayer. Before leaving, couples are encouraged to Make a Date for this session's HomeBuilders Project.

Parental Involvement

Involvement can mean different things to different parents. Some parents think they are involved with their adolescent children because they eat dinner together several nights a week or because they attend all their basketball games or volleyball matches.

If you want to help your child avoid the traps of adolescence, you will need to be committed to a higher level of involvement. Your children may not always welcome this type of involvement, and it may feel uncomfortable at times.

As a group, discuss:

- What are ways to stay connected and involved with adolescent children, even when they display little interest in your involvement? What has worked for you?

Make a Date

Make a date with your spouse to meet before the next session to complete the HomeBuilders Project (starting on page 26). Your leader will ask at the next session for you to share one aspect of this experience.

DATE
_____

TIME
_____

LOCATION
_____

Parent to Parent

During the next five sessions we will examine five of the hottest issues you will face with your teenagers:

- Peer pressure
- Sex
- Dating
- Media
- Substance abuse

In each session we'll talk about why each trap is particularly dangerous for teenagers, and we'll challenge you with some biblical convictions to build into your teenagers.

For now we'll leave you with some information that we've gleaned from our experience raising six teenagers:

1. Never underestimate the capacity for your teenagers to make foolish choices.

2. Staying involved in the life of your teenagers may be the most demanding and courageous commitment you can make as a parent.

3. Involvement means not losing heart when you don't see immediate results.

4. Never assume that your teenagers will learn all they need to walk in the truth through the influence of church, youth group, or a Christian school. Your role is critical.

5. Your example will speak louder than your words.

HOMEBUILDERS PROJECT   6 0   M I N U T E S

As a Couple [10 minutes]

Start your date by answering these questions:

When you were the same age as your teenager (if you have more than one teen, go with the age of your youngest)...

- How did you wear your hair?
- Who is someone you had a major crush on?
- Who was your favorite singer or band?

- What is one dream you had for your future?
- Do you think your teen is more like you were or more like your spouse was at the same age?

Individually [20 minutes]

1. What is one way you were challenged by the first session of this study?

2. What expectations do you have for this study?

3. In the group discussion, we talked about the importance of determining your convictions on the key issues your child will face as a teenager. Following is a list of a number of these issues. Review the list and evaluate how well you think you have developed convictions in each of these areas.

Rate yourself by giving yourself one of two marks:

- Y (for yes) if you can articulate a clear conviction for each issue
- N (for no) if you cannot

Using the same marks, also rate yourself on how you are doing in shaping your child's convictions in these areas. Remember that for something to be a conviction, you must think it is so true that you will take a stand for it regardless of the consequences.

Developed Own Convictions	*Shaping Child's Convictions*
Peer pressure ___	Peer pressure ___
Biblical view of sex ___	Biblical view of sex ___
Dating guidelines ___	Dating guidelines ___
Media consumption ___	Media consumption ___
Dealing with anger ___	Dealing with anger ___
Appearance ___	Appearance ___
Deceit ___	Deceit ___
Substance abuse ___	Substance abuse ___
Pornography ___	Pornography ___
Lordship of Christ ___	Lordship of Christ ___
Other: _____ ___	Other: _____ ___
Other: _____ ___	Other: _____ ___

4. What issue would you identify for yourself as being the one you most need to develop stronger convictions? for your teen (or teens)?

Interact as a Couple [30 minutes]

1. Share your answers from the individual section. As you discuss your responses, be open, kind, and understanding. Make an effort to listen to each other without interrupting.

2. Discuss what you are currently doing to provide biblical and spiritual instruction to your children.

3. In addition to the things you are already doing, what else should you consider doing to help develop convictions within your children?

---

4. Close in prayer. Ask God for wisdom as you seek to help guide your teen through the traps of adolescence.

Be sure to check out the related Parent-Teen Interaction on page 104. It provides a great opportunity to get involved in your teen's life and talk about the traps of adolescence.

Peer Pressure

Your involvement in your teenager's life will help
your teen make wise choices in choosing friends and
in resisting unhealthy influence from peers.

W A R M • U P   15 M I N U T E S

Avoiding the Traps

For this exercise you will need a blindfold, six to
eight sheets of paper, some tape, and six to eight
objects to place on the floor. You can use chairs,
books, boxes, lamps, anything you want. On each
sheet of paper, write the name of one of the following
"traps" of adolescence:

- Sex
- Dating
- Substance abuse
- Peer pressure

- Media
- Attitude
- Pornography
- Appearance

Tape the sheets of paper to the different objects. Blindfold one person, and place him or her at one end of the room. Then situate the objects in the room in such a way that it is impossible to walk in a straight line from one end of the room to the other without running into one of the traps.

The object of this exercise is for a volunteer to try to walk blindfolded from one end of the room to the other without touching any of the objects. As the volunteer attempts to navigate this mini obstacle course, everyone should offer advice to the blindfolded person—loudly and simultaneously!

After the volunteer attempts to negotiate the obstacle course this way, try again. This time, one person should act as a guide—standing next to the blindfolded person and coaching him or her through the obstacle course while the group is silent.

When finished, discuss these questions:

- How would you compare this exercise to the world in which teens live?
- What does this exercise say about how the traps of adolescence can be avoided?

Project Report

Share one thing you learned from last session's HomeBuilders Project.

The Effects of Peer Pressure

Peer pressure is not just an issue for teenagers. How often do you compare what you have with what others have? Are you ever tempted to buy certain brands of cars or clothes because that's what your friends prefer? Are you ever hesitant to express your opinion because others may not agree? Peer pressure is inescapable for all of us. But for teenagers it is an especially dangerous trap.

If you have a large group, form smaller groups of about six people to answer the Blueprints questions. Unless otherwise noted, answer the questions in your subgroup. Before moving into the Wrap-Up section, have sub-groups report to the whole group the highlights from their discussion.

1. In high school, who or what group had the most influence on you? What effect did your peer group have on the kind of choices you made? If you can, give an example.

2. In what ways have you seen your child influenced—for good or for bad—by peers recently?

3. From your personal experience as a teen and from your observation as a parent, what are ways peers undermine—intentionally or unintentionally—the authority of parents?

Answer question 4 with your spouse. After answering, you may want to share an appropriate insight or discovery with the group.

4. Based on what you know about your child, his or her friends, and today's youth culture, in what areas do you feel your child may be likely to face the greatest amount of peer pressure in the next two to three years?

Bad Company, Good Company

In our opening session we discussed the need to form convictions based on God's Word. Remember that having a conviction "is being so thoroughly convinced that something is absolutely true that you take a stand for it regardless of the consequences."

5. Read the following Bible passages:

- Psalm 1:1-3
- Proverbs 13:20
- 1 Corinthians 15:33

What guidance do you find in these verses that can help you form or solidify a biblical conviction about peer pressure?

6. Even in the best of circumstances, bad company seems to corrupt good company. Why do you think this is?

7. Read Ecclesiastes 4:9-12 and Hebrews 10:24. In what way can peer pressure be good for your teen?

HomeBuilders Principle:
The friends your teenagers choose play a critical role in the type of people they become.

Your Involvement

8. When your child was younger (preschool/elementary age), what role did you play in helping them select friends?

9. How does the role of parents in helping choose friends often change as a child enters and proceeds through adolescence?

10. Do you agree or disagree with the following statement? Explain.

It's important for adolescent children to have the freedom to choose their own friends.

Relating to Your Teenagers

11. In what ways can a strong relationship with your child influence how he or she responds to negative peer pressure? If you can, give an example.

12. What ideas have you heard of or tried to help your child find the right friends?

Negative Influences

Consider the following scenario:

You have a fourteen-year-old daughter, and you notice that she's been picking up some bad habits. She's starting to use rougher language, and she's increasingly acting disrespectful and sarcastic. It doesn't seem coincidental to you that this different behavior seemed to begin shortly after she began spending time with a couple of new friends. You question if these friends are a positive influence on her, but you've never even had the chance to meet them.

- In two groups—men and women—take a few minutes to discuss what steps, as a concerned mom or dad, you would take. Then each group should have a spokesperson report the approaches his or her group identified.

Make a Date

Make a date with your spouse to meet before the next session to complete this session's HomeBuilders Project. Your leader will ask at the next session for you to share one aspect of this experience.

Parent to Parent

Children face many traps as they move into adolescence, but it's no accident that we focused on peer pressure first. It's important for children to learn how to make choices based on biblical convictions rather than on what other people pressure them to do. If your child learns to stand strong against negative peer pressure, he or she will have a much greater chance of avoiding the other traps we will be discussing.

1. Never underestimate the power of peer pressure on your children.

2. Never assume that the Christian friends of your children are all good influences.

3. Never assume that other Christian families have the same standards as you.

4. Never assume that a friend who has been "good" through elementary school and junior high or middle school will continue to stay that way.

5. Never assume that your ability to discern the truth is greater than your child's ability to deceive you.

At times you will be tempted to think you're being too harsh by being involved in helping your child find good friends. Don't back off! The ability to stand against negative peer pressure will be used by God to embed convictions, courage, and a stand-alone faith that will help your child become a difference-maker for good in our culture.

HOMEBUILDERS PROJECT   6 0   M I N U T E S

As a Couple [10 minutes]

Start this date by reflecting back to when you were in high school.

- How would you describe what you were like as a freshman?
- Who was your best friend? Was he or she generally a good or bad influence on you? Explain.
- What kind of influence were you on your friends?
- Who was someone you looked up to as a role model?

Individually [20 minutes]

1. Review Session Two. What was the main thing you came away with from the group meeting?

2. How would you say you handle peer pressure now, as an adult? How well would you say your spouse generally handles peer pressure?

3. What are some examples of positive and negative peer pressure in your life?

4. How have you seen your child respond to peer pressure up until now? Be specific.

5. Who are the best friends of your child? Make a list.

6. How would you evaluate the friends your child has right now? What friends are a good influence, and what friends are not? Why?

7. What action steps for the trap of peer pressure do you want to apply to your life and to your parenting approach?

Interact as a Couple [30 minutes]

1. Share your answers from the individual section.

2. If you identified any problems or potential problems with your child's peer relationships, discuss what you can or should do. If you are comfortable with your child's current peer relationships, discuss what you can do to help support and encourage your child in continuing to make good relationship choices.

3. Discuss the convictions you would like your child to have for the trap of peer pressure. Review the sample convictions that follow, and then start your own list.

- Teen's Conviction 1: The friends I choose will have a big influence on the kind of person I become.

- Teen's Conviction 2: I will not assume that Christian friends will always be a good influence on me.

- Teen's Conviction 3: To help me stand strong against peer pressure, I will try to decide in advance how I will respond to key life choices like drug and alcohol use or sexual temptations.

4. Close in prayer, with each of you completing the following sentence: "Dear God, my specific prayer for our child and his or her friends is…"

Be sure to check out the related Parent-Teen Interaction on page 105. It provides a great opportunity to get involved in your teen's life and talk about the trap of peer pressure.

Sex

You can help your teenagers avoid the trap of sex by challenging them to a high standard of purity and innocence.

W A R M • U P   15   M I N U T E S

Sensual Saturation

For this exercise you will need a variety of popular magazines—current or old—that your children may look through. These could be weeklies such as People, Newsweek, or Time, but if possible have magazines that are geared primarily toward men, women, or teenagers (such as GQ, Cosmopolitan, and Seventeen).

Depending on how many magazines you have, break into subgroups of two to four people with each group assigned a different magazine or two. In your group, go through your magazine(s) looking for examples of advertisements, articles, or photos your group feels are inappropriately sexually suggestive. After each group reports its findings, discuss these questions:

- Were you surprised by what you found? Explain.
- What philosophy do you think lies behind many of these messages?
- How do you think children, especially teenagers, are affected by these types of messages?

Project Report

Share one thing you learned from last session's HomeBuilders Project.

BLUEPRINTS   60 MINUTES

Beyond the Birds and the Bees

If you have a large group, form smaller groups of about six people to answer the Blueprints questions. Unless otherwise noted, answer the questions in your subgroup. Before moving into the Wrap-Up section, have subgroups report to the whole group the highlights from their discussion.

1. As a teen, what was your primary source of sex education?

2. Would you want your children to learn about sex the same way you did? Why?

Case Study

It was not hard for Richard to notice that his fourteen-year-old son, Nathan, had developed an interest in the opposite sex. Nathan kept up lively correspondence on the Internet with different girls from his school, and had begun calling girls on the phone.

Richard had told Nathan about "the birds and the bees" several years earlier. But now he wanted to talk with Nathan about much more—the temptations that he was facing as a young teenage boy, and the choices he would face about sex and dating.

It was just so hard to build up the courage to bring up the subject. "He probably wouldn't listen to me anyway," Richard thought, "just like I never listened to my parents when it came to sex."

Of course, now he realized he should have followed his parents' advice. Richard's first sexual experience came at age seventeen, and he slept with a number of other women over the next few years. His life had changed when he became a Christian during his senior year of college, and he had remained faithful to Nathan's mother. Yet he still felt a lot of guilt about his lifestyle during those years before he came to Christ. He felt like a hypocrite. How could he challenge Nathan to standards he had never come close to meeting when he was a teenager?

3. Many parents today face similar issues as Richard as they deal with the choices they made in the past. What advice would you give to Richard?

4. What are the potential consequences if children aren't properly taught or guided (or if teens disregard the instruction they have received) about sex?

Answer question 5 with your spouse. After answering, you may want to share an appropriate insight or discovery with the group.

5. What have you done so far to teach your child about sex and to guide him or her in making responsible moral choices?

HomeBuilders Principle:
Parents must take responsibility to teach and model biblical morality and purity.

What Does God's Word Say About Sex?

In a world of shifting standards regarding sexual relations, we need to base our convictions on the truth found in the Bible.

6. With each couple selecting one or more of the following Scripture passages, read your verses with your spouse, and discuss what insight these verses give about what the Bible says about sex. Then share your verses with the group, and report on your insights.

- Genesis 1:27-28
- Genesis 2:22-25
- Proverbs 5:18-19
- Song of Songs 2:2-7
- 1 Corinthians 7:2-4
- Hebrews 13:4

7. Why do you think God reserves sex for a man and woman to enjoy in the context of marriage? List as many reasons as you can.

Where Do You Draw the Line?

8. If you were to ask a cross section of parents in your community, "What are you teaching your children about sex and morality?" what do you think the most common answers would be?

9. On a recent television news report about churches that are teaching abstinence to their teens, one teenage girl said she would remain a virgin until she

SESSION THREE • SEX

49

was married. But in the next breath she said that heavy kissing and petting were OK as long as she didn't engage in the act of sexual intercourse. What do you think of this view?

10. What do the following passages tell us about God's standard for sexual purity?

- 1 Corinthians 6:18

- Ephesians 5:3

- 1 Thessalonians 4:3-5

11. Read Romans 16:19. What do you think it means to be "innocent about what is evil"?

12. Practically, what are a few specific things you can do to protect the innocence of your children in today's sex-obsessed culture?

HomeBuilders Principle:
God calls us to protect not only the virginity of our children, but also their purity and innocence.

W R A P • U P   15   M I N U T E S

Debate

Pair up with another person for a short, friendly debate. Choose one of the following statements, and flip a coin to see which of you will, for the purposes of this exercise, agree with the statement and who will disagree. Discuss the statement you selected, taking turns to "argue" your assigned side. After five minutes, each pair should report to the group, sharing the best argument your partner made during your debate.

- "I don't see anything wrong with kissing, or even French kissing, before marriage. But that's where I draw the line."
- "I am going to make my first kiss my wedding kiss."

Make a Date

Make a date with your spouse to meet before the next session to complete this session's HomeBuilders Project.

DATE

TIME

LOCATION

Parent to Parent

When parents make mistakes in teaching children about sex, it's usually not because they were too involved. Instead the parents made some dangerous assumptions that their children's convictions and standards were more firmly in place than they were.

Even if you've done a great job of instructing your children about the biological facts of sex, you need to finish the process with moral training. Of all the discussions we've had in our family about sex, probably ninety-five percent of them have concerned character issues.

Remember:

1. Don't let your own mistakes in this area prevent you from fulfilling your responsibility as a parent.

2. If you don't teach your children about sex, and about biblical morality, the world will.

3. It is better to challenge your children to a high standard (with grace) than to no standard at all.

4. Just because a child has made good choices in this area in the past doesn't guarantee he or she will continue to take a strong stand. The pressure is relentless.

This is why your ongoing involvement in your teen's life is so important. You need to have the type of relationship where your child feels free to talk to you about these sensitive subjects. And your child needs to know that if he or she fails, you will show plenty of love and grace even if you are disappointed with the choice made.

As a Couple [10 minutes]

Start this project by watching some TV. (If you are out for this date, do this portion of the project later at home.) Spend up to five minutes watching a show, preferably a current sitcom on one of the primary networks. Then discuss these questions:

- What types of references to sex were there? What, if anything, did you see that you feel was inappropriate sexual content?

- What effect or influence do you think inappropriate sexual content on TV has on your teen?

- How comfortable are you having your teen regularly exposed to material you find objectionable? What can or should you do about this?

Individually [20 minutes]

1. If you are dealing with guilt concerning past sexual sin, this would be a good time to seek forgiveness and cleansing from God. (If you are uncertain how to handle this issue, or how much to divulge to your spouse, we suggest seeking Christian counsel from a spiritually mature individual, pastor, or counselor.)

Here are three steps we encourage you to take:

1. Read Psalm 103:11-14, which speaks of God's forgiveness of our sins.
2. Pray, confessing your sin to God.
3. Read 1 John 1:9 as a way to claim the assurance that you've been forgiven.

If you have questions or doubts about whether you have a personal relationship with God, read the article "Our Problems, God's Answers" starting on page 120.

2. What did this session reveal to you—good or bad—about how you are doing in giving your teen guidance for the trap of sex?

3. What are the biggest concerns you have about the influences on your child in regard to the trap of sex?

Questions 4-7 are designed to help you solidify or for-mulate your convictions about the trap of sex.

4. What would you say is the purpose of sex?

5. How would you reply if your preteen or teenager asked you, "Why is it wrong to have sex before marriage?"

6. How would you rate or evaluate yourself on how your personal example—your media and entertain-ment choices, as well as the way you treat your spouse and others of the opposite sex—communicates to your teen the principle of sexual purity?

7. Many parents do not get specific with their teenagers about how far they should go with the oppo-site sex before marriage. Review the following list. Where do you think your child should draw the line, and why?

Holding hands

Being alone

Hugging

Kissing

French kissing

Kissing while lying down

Touching private areas

Sexual stimulation

Sexual intercourse

Interact as a Couple [30 minutes]

1. Talk through your responses to questions 2-7 from the individual section.

2. Discuss what standards you want to set for your preteen or teen as he or she relates to the opposite sex. Review the sample convictions, and then start your list.

- Teen's Conviction 1: I will believe and trust in God's view of sex.
- Teen's Conviction 2: I will maintain my purity and innocence until I am married.

3. Consider what things about sex you need to communicate to your child. Talk about when and where these issues should be addressed, and by whom.

4. Pray, asking God to give you wisdom, discernment, and courage as you seek to communicate and educate your child about sex, and influence the standards he or she adopts.

Be sure to check out the related Parent-Teen Interaction on page 107. It provides a great opportunity to interact with your teenagers about the trap of sex.

Dating

One of the greatest challenges for parents is to set solid standards for their teens as they begin dating.

W A R M • U P   15   M I N U T E S

Dating Questionnaire

Take a few minutes to answer the following questions with your spouse, and then report your answers to the group.

• What is a date? How would you define the word?

• What do you think is the purpose of dating?

• How old should your children be to date? Why?

Project Report

Share one thing you learned from last session's
HomeBuilders Project.

BLUEPRINTS   60 MINUTES

Cultural Context

As you may have discovered during the Warm-Up,
part of the challenge of discussing "dating" is that the
term means different things to different people, and
even to different generations. For example, let's say
your daughter receives a phone call from a boy that
she knows from school. He asks her to go to the
school's winter dance. He picks her up at your home,
takes her to the dance, and drives her home. You
might call this a "date," but your daughter may insist
that it is not. Many young people only use the term

"dating" to mean a more serious relationship.

For the benefit of our discussion, keep the following two things in mind: (1) Every culture develops some type of system for young people to learn how to relate to the opposite sex and to find someone to marry, and (2) it is highly likely that most, if not all, of your sons and daughters will eventually get married.

As parents, we should evaluate the system in our culture (what we generally call "dating") and determine how well it works with our own goals for teaching and training our children about relating to the opposite sex.

1. What are some of the pros and cons of how young people today spend time and form relationships with the opposite sex?

If you have a large group, form smaller groups of about six people to answer the Blueprints questions. Unless otherwise noted, answer the questions in your subgroup. Before moving into the Wrap-Up section, have subgroups report to the whole group the highlights from their discussion.

2. What do you find positive or negative about the way dating relationships are portrayed in movies and on TV?

3. An issue confronting parents in the adolescent years is boyfriend/girlfriend relationships. What can be some of the drawbacks of this type of attachment?

Your Responsibility

Answer questions 4 through 6 with your spouse. After answering, you may want to share an appropriate insight or discovery with the group.

4. What type of training do you think your child needs in order to learn how to relate to the opposite sex?

5. What are the key character qualities or convictions you want your child to have as he or she begins to spend time with friends of the opposite sex and date?

6. What type of training does your child need to become a good spouse?

7. Review the following list of some ways parents can get involved in their teenagers' lives as they begin to date:

- Requiring your children to show responsibility in different areas (such as completing household chores and keeping up with homework) before being allowed to date

- Volunteering to be a chaperone for dances and other school functions

- Encouraging your children to use your home as a gathering place for them and their friends

- Making an effort to meet and get to know the opposite-sex friends your children are spending time with

- Making an effort to meet the parents of those friends

- Interviewing those who go on dates with your children to challenge them to high standards

- Asking your children on a regular basis how they are living up to the standards they've committed to

Which of these things have you tried, and with what result? What are some other ideas?

8. What possible dangers might you be risking if you don't get involved in ways like the ideas mentioned in the previous list?

HomeBuilders Principle:
Your teenagers need your training, guidance, and ongoing involvement as they approach the issue of dating relationships.

Setting Standards

There are a number of issues for you to consider as you set standards for your teenagers. These include:

- Character qualities they should display in order to earn the right to date
- Whether they should have boyfriend/girlfriend relationships
- Dealing with sexual temptation
- When to allow them to begin activities with the opposite sex—in groups and on a one-on-one date
- Who they should date
- How they should honor parents—their own and

those of the people they date

9. What, if any, standards did your parents have for you when you began to date? What impact did these standards, or lack thereof, have on your dating behavior?

Key Issues

Let's look closer at three of the key issues surrounding dating:

- Who they should date
- Dealing with temptation
- Honoring parents

Who they should date

10. Read 2 Corinthians 6:14-15. How would you apply this passage to your teens' dating relationships?

Dealing with temptation

11. Read 2 Timothy 2:22. In light of this verse, how would you complete the following sentence: "Pursuing righteousness in dating relationships means that my teen should…"

Honoring parents

12. Read Exodus 20:12. In what practical ways would you like your children to show honor and respect to you and to the parents of those they date?

HomeBuilders Principle:
Teenagers should be encouraged to "pursue righteousness" in dating relationships and to date those who share similar convictions.

What Would You Do?

It's one thing to talk about setting standards; it's quite another to implement and enforce them. Let's get practical by looking at some real-life situations. With your spouse, select one of the following scenarios to discuss, then report your response to the group.

- Your daughter, who just turned fourteen, is asked by a seventeen-year-old boy to go to a movie. What would you do?

- Your fifteen-year-old son has a girlfriend the same age. They want to spend all their time together. They talk for at least an hour on the phone each night, and she visits often at your home. You become concerned that they are becoming too emotionally attached. What would you do?

- Your sixteen-year-old son starts dating a girl he met at school. You don't know her or her family, and from the description you've heard from other

parents, you wonder if she is a good influence.
What would you do?

- You return home with your spouse late one night,
  and you see your seventeen-year-old daughter
  locked in a passionate embrace with her
  boyfriend in his car. What do you do? (Would
  your response be the same if it were your son you
  saw with his girlfriend?)

Make a Date

Make a date with your spouse to meet before the next
session to complete this session's HomeBuilders
Project.

DATE

TIME

LOCATION

Parent to Parent

For us, dating or courting is a small part of the overall process of determining God's will for discovering
our life partner in marriage. In our family the focus
has not been on dating, but more on training our
teens in their character and in how to develop a

---

relationship with the opposite sex.

In forming our own convictions as parents about dating, it's not good enough for us just to back off a step or two from what the world says is acceptable. Too many teenagers are being permanently scarred by the dating game. We want to challenge you to develop a fresh approach, prayerfully determine your limits, and train your child to hold fast to them.

A few tips:

1. When setting boundaries for your children, do not underestimate the power of the sex drive.

2. Don't assume a Christian child will be able to make wise choices about who to date.

3. Don't listen to the culture when it tells you to stay out of the dating lives of your children.

This is a great opportunity for you to train your children in so many important areas—relating to the opposite sex, choosing a spouse, dealing with temptation, and more. Don't let it pass you by...get involved!

As a Couple [10 minutes]

Discuss the following:

- How old were you when you went on your first date? How old was your date?
- Who was your first date? What did you do?
- Overall, was dating generally a good or bad experience for you? Explain. What could have made it better?

Individually [20 minutes]

1. Look back through this session. What are the main points on dating that seem most relevant to your family situation?

2. What was a standard regarding dating that your spouse or in-laws had that you appreciated?

3. What aspects of dating do you feel you handled well when dating your spouse?

4. What dating mistakes would you like to see your children avoid?

5. If your child marries, what qualities would you want to be most evident in your son's or daughter's future spouse?

6. What is one thing you could do in a more intentional way to train or model to your teen how to be an excellent spouse?

Family Dating Guidelines

7. What do you think would be some reasonable standards to set in each of the following areas? Write down one standard under each item listed.

- Character qualities they should display in order to earn the right to date

- Whether they should have boyfriend/girlfriend relationships

- Dealing with sexual temptation

- When to allow them to begin activities with the opposite sex—in groups and on a one-on-one date

- Who they should date

- How they should honor parents—their own and those of the people they date

Interact as a Couple [30 minutes]

1. Share your answers to questions 1-6 in the individual section.

2. Tell each other what you wrote down as "Family Dating Guidelines" under question 7 in the previous section. Discuss the benefits of having a formal list of dating guidelines. If you were to adopt a list of guidelines, what items do you agree need to be included?

3. Discuss the convictions you would like to see your teen form about dating. Review the sample convictions, and then write your own.

- Teen's Conviction 1: Until I am much older, I will concentrate on building friendships, not romantic emotional attachments, with the opposite sex.
- Teen's Conviction 2: I need to accept my parents' involvement and heed their judgment when it comes to issues surrounding time spent with the opposite sex.

- Teen's Conviction 3: I need to treat members of the opposite sex wisely and honorably.

4. Close in prayer. Pray specifically for each of your children and for the relationships in their lives.

Be sure to check out the related Parent-Teen Interaction on page 110. It provides a great opportunity to interact with your teenagers about the trap of dating.

Media

Teenagers need to develop discernment about the
type and amount of media they consume.

W A R M • U P   15   M I N U T E S

Media Log

Thinking back to yesterday, how much time did you
spend reading, watching, or listening to various types
of entertainment- or news-based media? Take a
minute to fill out the log below, based on your best
estimates, and then discuss the questions that follow.

Type	*Time*
Music/Radio	
TV/Movies	
Internet	
Newspapers/Magazines	
Books	
Video Games	
Other:	
TOTAL:	

- What was your total?

- How do you think the amount of media you consumed yesterday would compare with that of your teen?

- What do you see as good or bad about the variety of media you use on any given day?

Project Report

Share one thing you learned from last session's HomeBuilders Project.

BLUEPRINTS   60 MINUTES

Media Saturation

Each day we are bombarded by messages and offered an array of media choices—all competing for our time and attention. We need to take time to evaluate how this flood of media affects us—and our children.

There are two areas we need to focus on in evaluating media:

The time it takes

Its content

1. In what ways can too much exposure to media hurt your relationship with your children—especially teenagers?

If you have a large group, form smaller groups of about six people to answer the Blueprints questions. Unless otherwise noted, answer the questions in your subgroup. Before moving into the Wrap-Up section, have subgroups report to the whole group the highlights from their discussion.

2. How do you think it would affect your family if you took a drastic step to limit the use of media in your home? For example, what would happen if you

- abolished television (including videos and DVDs) for a week? a month? for good?

- limited the recreational use of the Internet (Web surfing, e-mailing friends, instant messaging) to one hour per week of "screen time" per person?

3. In what ways have you seen media content change since your childhood? What are some positive and negative changes you've observed?

Positive changes	*Negative changes*

4. Why do you think media can be such a trap for teenagers? How have you seen your teen affected by the content of the media he or she chooses to watch, read, or listen to?

HomeBuilders Principle:
Media must not replace relationships or relationship building in a family.

Worthless Things

Psalm 101:2-4 declares, "I will give heed to the blameless way. When will You come to me? I will walk within my house in the integrity of my heart. I will set no worthless thing before my eyes; I hate the work of those who fall away; it shall not fasten its grip on me" (NASB).

5. What, in your opinion, are examples from media of worthless things that should be avoided?

6. Read Colossians 2:8. How can the "hollow and deceptive" philosophies presented in the media undermine your faith and take you and your children captive?

7. Read Ephesians 4:17-19. How can the media we expose ourselves to work to harden our hearts toward God and dull our sensitivities?

Setting Standards

With such a bewildering array of media choices confronting us, and with so much filth just a click away, many parents are unprepared to handle the onslaught of media in their families. More than ever it is critical for us to set solid standards for ourselves and for our children.

8. Why do you think the media standards of parents—both Christians and non-Christians—vary so widely? Do you think parents are generally too strict or too lenient when it comes to the boundaries they set?

9. Read Philippians 4:8. Practically, how would you relate this passage to the issue of setting media standards for you and your children?

10. What effects—positive or negative—do you think your personal media habits have on your children?

Answer questions 10 and 11 with your spouse. After answering, you may want to share an appropriate insight or discovery with the group.

11. How good are you at keeping track of your teen's media interests and choices? How can you do a better job?

HomeBuilders Principle:
You must take responsibility to screen and set limits to the media used by your family.

Media-Free Family Time

As a group, brainstorm a list of things families could do together if they were to have a media-free family night or day—especially good parent-teen activity ideas.

Make a Date

Make a date with your spouse to meet before the next session to complete this session's HomeBuilders Project.

_____

DATE

_____

TIME

_____

LOCATION

Parent to Parent

Too many parents allow media to overwhelm their families because they have not thought through a clear, proactive plan for passing on clear convictions to their children. They haven't taken a good look at their own convictions, and often they haven't talked about guidelines for what their children should watch, read, and listen to.

One thing is certain: The media is becoming more and more pervasive in our lives. It can eat up our time, corrupt our morals, and erode our trust in the truth of God's Word. We encourage you to work carefully through this week's HomeBuilders Project and begin setting some clear convictions and guidelines.

Some truths to remember:

1. Never underestimate the influence of the media in your life or the lives of your children. It will continually pull you away from God.

2. Never underestimate the ability of your children to hide what they're doing.

3. Don't assume your children will not be lured to an Internet chat room, message board, or Web site that contains immoral or dangerous content.

4. Your children's "right to privacy" does not override your responsibilities as a parent. Don't be afraid to be a snoop—find out what media choices your children are making. Ask questions, look through their rooms, and install special software on your computer to monitor Web activity...do whatever it takes.

As a Couple [10 minutes]

Start this date by revisiting this session's Wrap-Up. What ideas did the group brainstorm that you would like to use with your family? Take some time to schedule and plan a media-free night or day for your family.

Decide:

- When will we have our media-free family time (date and duration)?

- What will we plan on doing during this time?

Individually [20 minutes]

1. What insight or concepts from this session do you most need to apply?

2. Revisit the Warm-Up exercise on page 75. Calculate how much time that you spent yesterday consuming various forms of media. And, if you can, make the same calculation for your teen(s).

3. How would you evaluate the amount of time you spent with media today for yourself (note with an S) and for your teenager(s) (note with child's initials)?

____ Way too much time

____ Too much time

____ Just about the right amount of time

____ Not enough time

____ Other: _____

4. What media-use patterns are you observing in your teen(s) that concern you?

5. What things could you or your teen(s) do—or do better—if you reduced the amount of time you gave to media?

6. Concerning your personal tastes in media, are you regularly watching, listening to, or reading material that you would be embarrassed to watch, read, or listen to with your preadolescent or teenager?

7. Read Titus 2:11-12. By what basis do we have the means to say no to things that are not good for us? What changes do you need to make in the media standards you have for yourself? for your children?

Interact as a Couple [30 minutes]

1. Share your answers from the individual section.

2. Based on what you have learned in this session and on your understanding of Scripture, discuss the convictions you want to claim in the area of media. Review the sample convictions, and then write your own.

- Teen's Conviction 1: I need to allow Jesus Christ to be Lord over all forms of media that I allow in my life.

- Teen's Conviction 2: I need to learn how to discern between good and evil in the media because what I allow to come into my mind can affect the way I think and live.
- Teen's Conviction 3: I need to stand firm and turn away from media temptations quickly.

3. Talk about specific guidelines you would like to have for your family in the media categories that follow, and how you can begin communicating these boundaries with your children.

- TV/Movies

- Internet

- Video Games

- Music/Radio

- Books/Magazines

- Other: _____

4. Pray about the standards you should have in the area of media. Ask God to give you wisdom in setting, modeling, and enforcing appropriate media standards.

For Extra Impact

Coming Attractions: Here's something you can do to help make informed choices about the movies, videos, and DVDs you watch. (Do this as a couple or as a family.)

Visit an Internet site that evaluates movies (such as www.screenit.com, www.gospelcom.net/preview, or www.MinistryandMedia.com). Look up a movie that you or your teen(s) want to see. Read the reviews, and then discuss these questions:

- How does having this information influence your choice?

- Do you find information like this helpful in making movie-viewing choices? Explain.

Be sure to check out the related Parent-Teen Interaction on page 113. It provides a great opportunity to interact with your teenagers about the trap of media.

Substance Abuse

Your connectedness with your teen, your integrity,
and your walk with God will help your child deal with
one of the deadliest traps of adolescence.

W A R M • U P   15   M I N U T E S

Addiction

Choose one of the following questions to answer, and
share with the group:

- How common was the use of drugs and alcohol in
  your high school? How do you think this com-
  pares with your child's school?

- Why do you think some parents find it uncomfortable or threatening to discuss the topic of
  substance abuse with their kids?

- If you can, tell the group about someone that you
  know who developed a problem with alcohol or
  drugs. How did this person get started? How did
  the problem affect his or her life and family?

Project Report

Share something you learned from last session's HomeBuilders Project.

BLUEPRINTS   60 MINUTES

Few families are untouched by the trap of substance abuse. Many people can name at least one relative— a brother, sister, parent, grandparent, aunt, uncle, cousin—who has a problem with alcohol, drugs, or painkillers. Add substances like cigarettes, inhalants, and diet pills, and you will find even more people struggling with some form of addiction—including many who don't know it.

If you have a large group, form smaller groups of about six people to answer the Blueprints questions. Unless otherwise noted, answer the questions in your subgroup. Before moving into the Wrap-Up section, have sub-groups report to the whole group the high-lights from their discussion.

One of the greatest fears for parents is that somehow their child will be caught in this trap.

Temptation

1. What were the illegal substances of choice when you were a teenager?

2. What do you think are the primary reasons that so many teenagers choose to experiment with alcohol, tobacco, or drugs?

3. As a group, see how many reasons you can list for why children should avoid these types of substances. Then read 1 Corinthians 6:19-20. What additional insight do you find in this passage?

4. What type of home environment do you feel would give your children the best opportunity to avoid falling into the trap of substance abuse?

Answer questions 4 and 5 with your spouse. After answering, you may want to share an appropriate insight or discovery with the group.

5. In your relationship with your teen, what do you think your child needs most from you at this stage in his or her life?

Connectedness

When dealing with this life-and-death issue, it is vitally important for parents to stay connected with their teenage children by knowing what's going on in their lives. Often parents don't know as much about their kids as they think they do. In one recent survey, for example, both parents and teens were asked what percentage of their child's life the parents knew about. The parents' answers ranged from 60 to 80 percent, while most of the children said 25 to 50 percent.

6. What do you think of the following actions parents could take to find out if their teenage children are sampling abusive substances? Rate each action on the agree-disagree scale, and then explain your answers to the group.

• Asking children if they're smoking, drinking, or taking drugs

Strongly disagree	Disagree	Agree	Strongly agree
1	2	3	4

- Waiting up for children to return home and smelling their breath before they go to bed

Strongly disagree	Disagree	Agree	Strongly agree
1	2	3	4

- Searching a child's room, clothes, or automobile

Strongly disagree	Disagree	Agree	Strongly agree
1	2	3	4

- Calling a parent whose child is hosting a party and asking if there will be alcohol or drugs

Strongly disagree	Disagree	Agree	Strongly agree
1	2	3	4

- Showing up uninvited at a teen party

Strongly disagree	Disagree	Agree	Strongly agree
1	2	3	4

- Asking other teenagers what they know about substance abuse in your child's school

Strongly disagree	Disagree	Agree	Strongly agree
1	2	3	4

HomeBuilders Principle:
To help your teenagers avoid abusive substances, you must stay connected—by knowing what is happening in their lives and by giving them plenty of attention, discipline, guidance, acceptance, and love.

Modeling Integrity

Throughout this study we have talked about your role as a model—a living picture of how to make choices with integrity. Psalm 101:2 tells us, "I will give heed to the blameless way...I will walk within my house in the integrity of my heart" (NASB).

7. Why is the example you set particularly important in the area of substance abuse?

8. Who had the greatest influence in your life to either use alcohol and drugs or avoid using them? Explain.

9. What are your personal standards regarding substance abuse? From the following list, pick one or two items, and tell the group about your personal standards for each.

- Alcohol
- Cigarettes
- Chewing Tobacco
- Marijuana
- Inhalants (adhesives, aerosols, solvents, and gases)
- Illicit Drugs (such as cocaine and ecstasy)
- Over-the-Counter Drugs (such as diet pills)
- Prescription Drugs (such as painkillers)
- Other: _____

Modeling a Walk With God

For many, substance abuse begins with an attempt to escape from reality or search for fulfillment from different things in life. But real life is found in a relationship with God. King David testifies to this in Psalm 16:11, praising God and declaring, "You have made known to me the path of life; you will fill me with joy in your presence, with eternal pleasures at your right hand."

10. If comfortable sharing, briefly tell the group how you came to be a Christ follower and how this relationship has changed your life.

11. Why is it critical for your teens to have a personal relationship with God as they negotiate not only the trap of substance abuse, but all the various traps of adolescence?

12. Read Psalm 78:5-8. How can you apply this passage to help ensure that your child will remain faithful to God? What things come to mind that you can do to model your trust in God before your children?

HomeBuilders Principle:
Teaching and modeling a rich love relationship with Jesus Christ will help your children develop their own trust in God and learn how to translate the wisdom they find in Scripture into their own daily lives and daily choices.

W R A P • U P   15   M I N U T E S

Reflections

As you come to the end of this course, take a few minutes to reflect on this experience. Review the following questions, and write down responses to the questions you can answer. Then relate to the group one or more of your answers.

• What has this group meant to you over the course of this study? Be specific.

• What is the most valuable thing that you have learned or discovered?

• How have you as a parent been changed or challenged?

• What would you like to see happen next for this group?

One of the great benefits of completing this HomeBuilders study with other parents is that you have been able to encourage each other to be consistently involved with your children as they move through adolescence. We challenge you to continue this involvement by doing three things:

- Pray regularly for each other and for your children.
- Keep in touch with each other. Contact each other for advice and encouragement as you face different issues with your children.
- Keep in touch with each other's children.

Other people can see things in your children—both good and bad—that you do not see. Make a special effort to tell your friends about good things that you've seen their children do. But also give your friends permission to pass on any concerns they may have. This is difficult to do. You will need to give each other a lot of grace in this area. But if you see a friend's child do something you know is not right, or if you see that child in a compromising situation, it may be more dangerous not to tell the parent.

Make a Date

Make a date with your spouse to meet in the next week to complete the last HomeBuilders Project of this study.

DATE

TIME

LOCATION

Parent to Parent

Though you may not realize it, this entire study has given you an opportunity to apply the words of Psalm 78:5-8 in your family. As you've studied the different traps of adolescence, we have exhorted you to put your confidence in God and the Bible, and to experience the Lord's guidance and leading. Your assignment as a parent is to teach your children to do the same.

Parenting is not an exact science. You can develop a wonderful relationship with your children, guide them with a good balance of love and discipline, and encourage them to form God-honoring convictions. And eventually your children will grow up, leave your home, and make their own choices.

In the end, your children need their own faith. They need to learn on their own to put their confidence in God. As a parent, your greatest privilege and greatest responsibility is showing them, on a daily basis, how to trust God in every area of life.

Some tips:

1. When it comes to substance abuse, your child's personal rights do not usurp your parental responsibility to snoop.

2. Don't become predictable with your teenager. Find fresh and surprising ways to ensure they are staying away from abusive substances.

3. Do not assume other parents share your standards about alcohol and drugs.

4. What you do in moderation, your children will be tempted to do in excess.

5. Nobody raises perfect children. In the end, they will make their own choices in life.

6. Our hope as parents is in God and his faithfulness.

HOMEBUILDERS PROJECT   6 0   M I N U T E S

As a Couple [10 minutes]

Congratulations—you've made it to the last project of this study! To start this date, reflect on what impact this course has had on you by discussing these questions:

- What has been the best part of this study for you?

- How has this study benefited your marriage?

- In what ways has this study helped you as a parent?

- What is something new you have learned or discovered about your spouse? about yourself? about your teen?

Individually [20 minutes]

1. What was the most important insight or lesson for you from this session?

2. Did your parents drink, smoke, or use drugs? What impact has the example of your parents had on you?

3. What, if any, substances that you regularly use might give your child the impression that you need this in order to be happy or to deal with life?

4. How comfortable would you be if your children were to adopt the same standards you have for the various substances that were discussed in this session? Why?

5. Do you have a child who you think may have tried or is likely to try alcohol, smoking, or drugs? Explain.

6. How would you assess the spiritual life of your chil- , dren? What do they need to develop or deepen in their relationship with God? (For more information on a personal relationship with God, read the article "Our Problems, God's Answers" starting on page 120.)

7. Thinking about this course overall, what is at least one point of action you've identified as something you want to do, stop doing, or change? What do you need to do to turn this action point into a reality?

Interact as a Couple [30 minutes]

1. Review and discuss your responses to the previous questions.

2. Review the following sample convictions regarding substance abuse, then work on starting your own list. Talk through the convictions you would like for your children to have and how best to communicate these standards.

- Teen's Conviction 1: I will honor and protect my own body because it "is a temple of the Holy Spirit" (1 Corinthians 6:19).
- Teen's Conviction 2: I will decide in advance what I will do when presented with the opportunity to smoke, drink alcohol, or use other drugs.

3. Evaluate things you can do to continue to strengthen your home. You may want to consider continuing the practice of setting aside time for date nights. You may also want to look at the list of ideas on page 119.

4. Close in prayer. Thank God for each other and for your children. Pray for God's wisdom and direction as you continue to seek to guide your teenagers.

Be sure to check out the related Parent-Teen Interaction on page 114. It provides a great opportunity to interact with your teenagers about the trap of substance abuse.

Please visit our Web site at www.familylife.com/homebuilders to give us your feedback on this study and to get information on other FamilyLife resources and conferences.

Parent-Teen Interactions

Interaction 1

The Traps of Adolescence

1. Take your teen or preteen out for a casual dinner or for dessert. After you've talked awhile, tell your teen about the HomeBuilders group that you are a part of. Describe the purpose of the course, which is to talk about how to help teenagers deal with the "traps of adolescence"—the key issues that all teenagers face (including you when you were that age). Issues such as peer pressure, sex, dating, media, and alcohol and drugs. Explain that part of the course involves a series of short projects for parents to complete with their teenagers (or preteens).

2. Tell your teenager, "For the next few minutes, think of me as a television or newspaper reporter conducting an interview with you to get your opinion on the key issues teenagers face."

3. Proceed to ask your teen the questions that follow. Avoid the temptation to talk, except to ask follow-up or clarifying questions. Encourage your teen to reply honestly, but let your teen know it's OK to "pass" on a question. The purpose of this first interaction is simply for you to listen to your son or daughter. This is your time to listen, not talk!

 • What would you say is the biggest problem teenagers face today?

- What does it take to be part of the "in" crowd at your school?

- When it comes to the subject of sex, is abstinence respected or made fun of? Explain.

- To you, what qualifies as a "date"? Give an example of what a date is and what a date isn't.

- Which musical artists or groups and radio stations are popular with the kids in your class?

- Would you say that the use of drugs at your school is higher than adults think or lower? What about alcohol use? Explain.

- Is there anything you would like to tell me about the issues teens face that I haven't asked?

Interaction 2

Peer Pressure

Use the following exercise to drive home a memorable lesson to your teen about how the friends we hang out with can have a big influence on our lives.

This interaction is based on the saying "One bad apple can spoil the whole barrel." Though this phrase no longer carries much meaning in a day when most of us buy apples by the bag and store them for only a short time, your teen won't forget the sight of what happens when you put a bad apple in with some good ones.

You will need three or four apples for this interaction. One of the apples needs to be damaged or bruised badly. (You can use other kinds of produce if you like. Tomatoes, lettuce, or an orange will work well. If you want the process to go as quickly as possible, use one of these kinds of produce.)

1. Show the apples or produce to your teen, and explain that the good apples represent teenagers who are making good choices when dealing with issues such as smoking, drinking, talking profanely, and being obedient to parents. Then ask, "With that in mind, what do you think the bruised apple represents?"

2. Tell your teenager that this illustration will show what happens when good apples spend too much time with bad apples. Put the apples together in a plastic bag—preferably one that has a self-seal, and with your teen find a warm, dark place to put the bag. Explain that you will come back later (in a few weeks or months—depending on how long you want this experiment to run) to see what happened.

3. Now have your teenager read 1 Corinthians 15:33 aloud. Ask, "What do you think this verse means? How does 'bad company' corrupt us?"

4. Ask, "What does this verse say to you about the type of friends you should choose?"

5. Talk with your teenager about the apples—other teens—in his or her life. Ask, "Who are some of your friends who influence you to do what is right?"

6. Together read Psalm 1:1-3. Ask, "What do you think it means to 'walk in the counsel of the wicked or stand in the way of sinners or sit in the seat of mockers'?"

7. Then ask, "Who are some people you know who are not the best influences?"

8. Be sure to note that it's impossible to live in our world without having friends who are not the best of influences. In fact, God calls us to be good influences on those "bad apples" by showing them the love of Christ. It's important, however, to make sure you are not allowing those bad influences to lead you into making poor choices.

9. Close your time in prayer. Ask God to give your teen the ability to discern the good apples and the bruised apples among his or her friends.

At a later date:

1. Check the apples to make sure they have all turned into a brownish, putrid mush. Then take your teenager with you to pull the apples out of where they have been stored. Ask, "How is this like what happens to us when we spend time with friends who are bad influences?"

2. Read 1 Corinthians 15:33 again, and ask your child, "Since we first talked about this subject, what additional things have you noticed about your friends? Who are the good influences, and who are not as good?"

Interaction 3

Sex

This interaction is divided into two sections. Part One is titled "What Does God Say About Sex?" It leads you through Scriptures and questions that give you the opportunity to talk with your teen about biblical standards on sexual purity.

Part Two, "Where Do You Draw the Line?" provides an object lesson on how easy it is to lose your innocence and then challenges your teen to verbalize his or her convictions. By doing this, you call your teen to accountability and create a future opportunity to talk further about this subject.

You are encouraged to do both parts. Depending on your schedule, you may want to complete these two parts on separate occasions.

Part One:
What Does God Say About Sex?

Note: Because this subject can be challenging to discuss with your teen, for the questions that follow, you may want to refer to your notes from the like questions (6, 7, 10, and 11) in Session Three (pages 48-50). There are also related commentary notes for these questions (numbered as 6, 7, 10, and 11) on pages 147-149.

1. Have your teen read each of the following Scriptures. After each one, ask: "What does this passage tell us about sex?"
  - Genesis 1:27-28
  - 1 Corinthians 7:2-4
  - Genesis 2:22-25
  - Hebrews 13:4
  - Proverbs 5:18-19

2. Ask, "Why do you think God reserves sex for a man and woman to enjoy in the context of marriage?"

3. Now have your teen read 1 Corinthians 6:18 and 1 Thessalonians 4:3-5. Ask, "What do these verses tell us about God's standards for sexual purity? What do you think it means to 'flee from sexual immorality' and 'avoid sexual immorality'?"

4. Read Romans 16:19. Ask, "What do you think it means to be 'innocent about what is evil'? How would you apply this to the subject of sexual morality?"

Part Two:
Where Do You Draw the Line?

For the following exercise, you need a needle and two balloons filled with water. Be sure to experiment beforehand to ensure you get the proper effect.

The first balloon should be small, so that when it is filled as full as you can get it while still being able to tie it off, it will burst when stuck with a pin. This demonstration will be used to illustrate how you can lose all your purity and innocence at once.

The second balloon should be strong and large enough so that when you fill it with water and actually prick it with a needle, it won't burst but will dribble out a drop or two, and if you squeeze it, it will shoot out a stream of water. Both the droplets and stream illustrate how sexual involvement can progress in a teenager's life.

1. Pick up the smaller water balloon first. Say, "This water balloon is filled with your sexual purity and innocence. This is all that you have. How much of it would you want to give away before you are married?"

2. Then say, "Let's say in a couple of years you meet the boy or girl of your dreams. The physical attraction is just too strong, and you decide just this once you're going to sleep with him or her. And what happens to your purity?" With your needle, tear a large hole in the water balloon so that all the water gushes out.

3. Now pick up the other water balloon. Then say, "That's one way to lose all of your purity and innocence. Now let's say that you date someone who just wants a little kiss, your first kiss and just a little bit of your innocence, and you agree." Hold the balloon up and pierce it with a needle. Say, "You think to yourself, 'What's the big deal? It's just a little drop. I'll never miss it.' "

4. Continue: "Then someone else comes along, and you date for awhile, and this person just wants a little droplet. He or she says, 'Let's make out in the car.' So you give the person a little more of your innocence…" Stick the needle in the balloon again a few more times.

5. "Then let's say you really like someone and you start to get serious. You decide it's OK to give even more of your purity and innocence away." Continue sticking the needle in the balloon until the water is all gone.

6. Say, "That relationship ends, and a few years later you finally meet the person you are going to marry." Then ask, "So now, as you approach your wedding night, how much of your purity will you have to give to the one you marry and spend the rest of your life with?"

7. Say, "That's how young people today are losing one of the most precious gifts that they can give to another human being; and they start by giving it away a drop at a time. Then they give away even more, and the holes get larger and it's no longer drops, but a small stream."

8. Finally, ask your teen, "Knowing what you now know about losing your purity and innocence, where would you draw the line about how far you are going to go with the opposite sex prior to marriage?"

--------------------| **Interaction 4** |--------------------

Dating

To talk with your teen about dating, we encourage you to take him or her out for a date. Often the father is the one who

Dating Questionnaire

1. What is the purpose of dating?

2. What is a date?

3. How old should you be to date? Why?

4. If you were a parent, when would you let your child begin dating?

5. When should you be able to double-date?

6. Would you choose to date only Christians? Why?

does this, especially with daughters, but you may want the mother to take out a son so he will hear a woman's perspective on this issue. Any combination will work. What's important is that you make the effort to connect with your teen on this issue; don't worry about saying everything perfectly.

1. Set the time you will take your teen out, and decide what the setting will be. A nice restaurant that is conducive to conversation without distractions like loud music or a bar works well. Call or write a note to your teen and make the invitation special. If you have never done this before, you may feel a bit awkward, but don't let this get in the way of meeting this important need in your teen.

   Before your date, give your teen a copy of the Dating Questionnaire (on page 111 of this interaction) to fill out prior to your date.

2. Dress like you are going on an important date. You are helping your child see and set a standard that will guide his or her social life. Besides, if you dress nicely, it will give the feeling of importance. Be sure to bring with you a Bible and this book, or write down on index cards the verses and questions from points 4 and 5.

3. As you begin your time together, simply remind your son or daughter that you need to discuss dating with him or her as part of your study. Tell your child that you want this date with you to be an example of how he or she should treat someone else or be treated on a date. Then ask how he or she answered the questions on the Dating Questionnaire.

4. After hearing your teen's answers to the Dating Questionnaire, read the following verses:
   - 2 Corinthians 6:14-15
   - Philippians 4:8

- 2 Timothy 2:22

Then discuss these questions:

- How do you think these verses should be applied to how we relate to the opposite sex?

- What standards do these verses point us to regarding your social life?

5. Together draft some guidelines that you and your teen agree should be a part of his or her social and dating life. Before you begin writing your standards, read Proverbs 1:8-9. Ask your teen, "How can this verse be applied by a teenager to the subject of dating?"

Interaction 5

Media

In this project you will talk with your teen about the different ways media affect us. You also will begin to teach him or her how to discern the different messages in the media. You will watch a television show together (or a movie, if you wish) and talk about the different philosophies promoted in the show and its advertisements.

Before doing this interaction, be sure you work through the HomeBuilders Project with your spouse and decide upon some family standards for media.

1. With your teen, create a list of all the different opportunities there are in your home to consume different types of media. Have your son or daughter write down a list of all the different types of media devices there are in the different rooms of your home—radios, televisions, VCRs, DVD players, CD players, books, magazines, computers, and video games. You and your teen may want to actually do a walk-through your home.

2. Ask your teen the following questions: "In what ways do you think all these media affect us? How do they affect our minds? How do they affect our family? How do they affect our walk with God?"

3. Have your teen read Psalm 101:2-4 and Philippians 4:8. Then ask, "How would you relate these passages to the issue of how we entertain ourselves with media?"

4. Ask, "What would you say is an example of a worthless or vile thing that your friends have seen or heard recently in the media?"

5. Ask, "What is an example of something you have seen or heard?"

6. Watch a television show (or a movie) together. Be sure not to skip the commercials.

7. When you're finished, ask, "What were some of the different values that this show promoted? How do these values compare to what we know to be true in God's Word?"

8. Then ask about the advertisements: "What were the ads trying to get us to do? What methods are they utilizing to persuade us? What values are they promoting? How do these values compare to what we know to be true in the Word of God?"

9. Share with your teen the guidelines you and your spouse discussed in the media session's HomeBuilders Project. Explain why you are setting these standards.

Interaction 6

Substance Abuse

1. For this interaction we suggest taking your teen to a meeting of Alcoholics Anonymous. This is the type of experience that

can leave a lasting impression.

There are thousands of AA chapters throughout the United States. To find one near you, look up "Alcoholics Anonymous" in the phone book, or talk to someone on staff at your church (or at your place of work). Ideally, find someone who is an AA member who would be willing to serve as your host for a visit to a meeting.

2. After attending the meeting, take your teen out and ask the following questions:
   • What were your impressions of the meeting?
   • Were you surprised by anything at the meeting?
   • What did you think of what the people there had to say?
   • How do you think their addictions have changed their lives?

3. Read Romans 12:1-2. Ask, "What do you think it means to present our bodies to the Lord as a living sacrifice that is holy and acceptable?"

4. Ask, "Practically, how can we present our bodies to the Lord? When or how often should this take place?"

5. Ask, "How do you think the concept of being a living sacrifice to the Lord applies to the subject of taking drugs or drinking alcohol?"

6. Conclude this outing by asking your teen to decide in advance what he or she would do in each of the following scenarios:
   • You are walking home from school, and a friend pulls out a cigarette. He asks you if you want one too. You say no, and he says, "Why don't you just try it? One little cigarette isn't going to hurt you." What do you do, and why?
   • A friend is having a small party with several other girls and boys from your high school. One of the girls brings in a cooler full of beer and starts handing them out. What do you do, and why?

For Extra Impact

1. Plan a time with your teenage children (in fact, you can include the entire family if you want) in which you do something active for at least four hours or more. Go out and play games, take a hike, go to the zoo, clean the yard together, play softball—anything to get good and dirty and sweaty. Whatever you do, make sure you have fun together!

2. Here's the catch: When you're finished, *do not take a bath or shower until the next day*! Continue with your other activities throughout the rest of the day. Talk about how it feels to be so dirty. Don't be in a hurry. Enjoy this interaction as a family. Make some jokes—have fun with this.

3. The following morning, before showers or baths, prepare a nice breakfast and, while you eat together, ask your family, "How has it felt to be so dirty for so long? What was it like trying to sleep last night?"

4. Ask, "What kind of things make the inside of our bodies dirty?"

5. Discuss, "How do these things make our bodies dirty?"

Where Do You Go From Here?

It is our prayer that you have benefited greatly from this study in the HomeBuilders Parenting Series. We hope that your marriage and home will continue to grow stronger as you both submit your lives to Jesus Christ and build according to his blueprints.

We also hope that you will begin reaching out to strengthen other marriages in your community and local church. Your church needs couples like you who are committed to building Christian marriages. A favorite World War II story illustrates this point very clearly.

The year was 1940. The French Army had just collapsed under Hitler's onslaught. The Dutch had folded, overwhelmed by the Nazi regime. The Belgians had surrendered. And the British Army was trapped on the coast of France in the channel port of Dunkirk.

Two hundred and twenty thousand of Britain's finest young men seemed doomed to die, turning the English Channel red with their blood. The Fuehrer's troops, only miles away in the hills of France, didn't realize how close to victory they actually were.

Any rescue seemed feeble and futile in the time remaining. A "thin" British Navy—"the professionals"—told King George VI that at best they could save 17,000 troops. The House of Commons was warned to prepare for "hard and heavy tidings."

Politicians were paralyzed. The king was powerless. And the Allies could only watch as spectators from a distance. Then as the doom of the British Army seemed imminent, a strange fleet appeared on the horizon of the English Channel—the wildest assortment of boats perhaps ever assembled in history.

Trawlers, tugs, scows, fishing sloops, lifeboats, pleasure craft, smacks and coasters, sailboats, even the London fire-brigade flotilla. *Each ship was manned by civilian volunteers—English fathers sailing to rescue Britain's exhausted, bleeding sons.*

William Manchester writes in his epic book, *The Last Lion,* that even today what happened in 1940 in less than twenty-four hours seems like a miracle—not only were all of the British soldiers rescued, but 118,000 other Allied troops as well.

Today the Christian home is much like those troops at Dunkirk. Pressured, trapped, and demoralized, it needs help. Your help. The Christian community may be much like England—we stand waiting for politicians, professionals, even for our pastors to step in and save the family. But the problem is much larger than all of those combined can solve.

With the highest divorce rate of any nation on earth, we need an all-out effort by men and women who are determined to help rescue the exhausted and wounded casualties of today's families. We need an outreach effort by common couples with faith in an uncommon God.

May we challenge you to invest your lives in others? You have one of the greatest opportunities in history—to help save today's families. By starting a HomeBuilders group, you can join couples around the world who are building and rebuilding hundreds of thousands of homes with a new, solid foundation of a relationship with God.

Will You Join Us in "Touching Lives...Changing Families"?

The following are some practical ways you can make a difference in families today:

1. Gather a group of four to eight couples, and lead them through the six sessions of this HomeBuilders study, *Guiding Your Teenagers*. (Why not consider challenging others in your church or community to form additional HomeBuilders groups?)

2. Commit to continue building your marriage and home by doing another course in the HomeBuilders Parenting Series or by leading a study in the HomeBuilders Couples Series.

3. An excellent outreach tool is the film *JESUS*, which is available on video. For more information, contact FamilyLife at 1-800-FL-TODAY.

4. Host a dinner party. Invite families from your neighborhood to your home, and as a couple share your faith in Christ.

5. Reach out and share the love of Christ with neighborhood children.

6. If you have attended the Weekend to Remember conference, why not offer to assist your pastor in counseling couples engaged to be married, using the material you received?

For more information about any of the above ministry opportunities, contact your local church, or write:

FamilyLife
P.O. Box 8220
Little Rock, AR 72221-8220
1-800-FL-TODAY
www.familylife.com

Our Problems, God's Answers

●

Every couple eventually has to deal with problems in marriage. Communication problems. Parenting issues. Money problems. Difficulties with sexual intimacy. These issues are important to cultivating a strong, loving relationship with your spouse. Home-Builders Bible studies are designed to help you strengthen your marriage and family in many of these critical areas.

Part One: The Big Problem

One basic problem is at the heart of every other problem in every marriage, and it's a problem we can't help you fix. No matter how hard you try, this is one problem that is too big for you to deal with on your own.

The problem is separation from God. If you want to experience marriage the way it was designed to be, you need a vital relationship with the God who created you and offers you the power to live a life of joy and purpose.

And what separates us from God is one more problem—sin. Most of us have assumed throughout our lives that the term "sin" refers to a list of bad habits that everyone agrees are wrong. We try to deal with our sin problem by working hard to become better people. We read books to learn how to control our anger, or we resolve to stop cheating on our taxes.

But in our hearts, we know our sin problem runs much deeper than a list of bad habits. All of us have rebelled against God. We have ignored him and have decided to run our own lives in a way that makes sense to us. The Bible says that the God who created us wants us to follow his plan for our lives. But because of our sin problem, we think our ideas and plans are better than his.

- *"For all have sinned and fall short of the glory of God"* (Romans 3:23).

What does it mean to "fall short of the glory of God"? It means that none of us has trusted and treasured God the way we should. We have sought to satisfy ourselves with other things and have treated those things as more valuable than God. We have gone our own way. According to the Bible, we have to pay a penalty for our sin. We cannot simply do things the way we choose and hope it will all be OK with God. Following our own plan leads to our destruction.

- *"There is a way that seems right to a man, but in the end it leads to death"* (Proverbs 14:12).
- *"For the wages of sin is death"* (Romans 6:23a).

The penalty for sin is that we are forever separated from God's love. God is holy, and we are sinful. No matter how hard we try, we cannot come up with some plan, like living a good life or even trying to do what the Bible says, and hope that we can avoid the penalty.

God's Solution to Sin

Thankfully, God has a way to solve our dilemma. He became a man through the person of Jesus Christ. He lived a holy life, in perfect obedience to God's plan. He also willingly died on a cross to pay our penalty for sin. Then he proved that he is more powerful than sin or death by rising from the dead. He alone has the power to overrule the penalty for our sin.

- *"Jesus answered, 'I am the way and the truth and the life. No one comes to the Father except through me' "* (John 14:6).

- *"But God demonstrates his own love for us in this: While we were still sinners, Christ died for us"* (Romans 5:8).

- *"Christ died for our sins...he was buried...he was raised on the third day according to the Scriptures...he appeared to Peter, and then to the Twelve. After that, he appeared to more than five hundred"* (1 Corinthians 15:3-6).

- *"For the wages of sin is death, but the gift of God is eternal life in Christ Jesus our Lord"* (Romans 6:23).

The death of Jesus has fixed our sin problem. He has bridged the gap between God and us. He is calling all of us to come to him and to give up our own flawed plan for how to run our lives. He wants us to trust God and his plan.

Accepting God's Solution

If you agree that you are separated from God, he is calling you to confess your sins. All of us have made messes of our lives because we have stubbornly preferred our ideas and plans over his. As a result, we deserve to be cut off from God's love and his care for us. But God has promised that if we will agree that we have rebelled against his plan for us and have messed up our lives, he will forgive us and will fix our sin problem.

- *"Yet to all who received him, to those who believed in his name, he gave the right to become children of God"* (John 1:12).

- *"For it is by grace you have been saved, through faith—and this not from yourselves, it is the gift of*

God—not by works, so that no one can boast" (Ephesians 2:8-9).

When the Bible talks about receiving Christ, it means we acknowledge that we are sinners and that we can't fix the problem ourselves. It means we turn away from our sin. And it means we trust Christ to forgive our sins and to make us the kind of people he wants us to be. It's not enough to just intellectually believe that Christ is the Son of God. We must trust in him and his plan for our lives by faith, as an act of the will.

Are things right between you and God, with him and his plan at the center of your life? Or is life spinning out of control as you seek to make your way on your own?

You can decide today to make a change. You can turn to Christ and allow him to transform your life. All you need to do is to talk to him and tell him what is stirring in your mind and in your heart. If you've never done this before, consider taking the steps listed here:

- Do you agree that you need God? Tell God.

- Have you made a mess of your life by following your own plan? Tell God.

- Do you want God to forgive you? Tell God.

- Do you believe that Jesus' death on the cross and his resurrection from the dead gave him the power to fix your sin problem and to grant you the gift of eternal life? Tell God.

- Are you ready to acknowledge that God's plan for your life is better than any plan you could come up with? Tell God.

- Do you agree that God has the right to be the Lord and master of your life? Tell God.

> *"Seek the Lord while he may be found;*
> *call on him while he is near"*
> (Isaiah 55:6).

Following is a suggested prayer:

Lord Jesus, I need you. Thank you for dying on the cross for my sins. I receive you as my Savior and Lord. Thank you for forgiving my sins and giving me eternal life. Make me the kind of person you want me to be.

Does this prayer express the desire of your heart? If it does, pray it right now, and Christ will come into your life, as he promised.

Part Two: Living the Christian Life

For a person who is a follower of Christ—a Christian—the penalty for sin is paid in full. But the effect of sin continues throughout our lives.

- *"If we claim to be without sin, we deceive ourselves and the truth is not in us"* (1 John 1:8).

- *"For what I do is not the good I want to do; no, the evil I do not want to do—this I keep on doing"* (Romans 7:19).

The effects of sin carry over into our marriages as well. Even Christians struggle to maintain solid, God-honoring marriages. Most couples eventually realize that they can't do it on their own. But with God's help, they can succeed. The Holy Spirit can have a huge impact in the marriages of Christians who live constantly, moment by moment, under his gracious direction.

Self-Centered Christians

Many Christians struggle to live the Christian life in their own strength because they are not allowing God to control their lives. Their interests are self-directed, often resulting in failure and frustration.

- *"Brothers, I could not address you as spiritual but as worldly—mere infants in Christ. I gave you milk, not solid food, for you were not yet ready for it. Indeed, you are still not ready. You are still worldly. For since there is jealousy and quarreling among you, are you not worldly? Are you not acting like mere men?"* (1 Corinthians 3:1-3).

The self-centered Christian cannot experience the abundant and fruitful Christian life. Such people trust in their own efforts to live the Christian life: They are either uninformed about—or have forgotten—God's love, forgiveness, and power. This kind of Christian

- has an up-and-down spiritual experience.

- cannot understand himself—he wants to do what is right, but cannot.

- fails to draw upon the power of the Holy Spirit to live the Christian life.

Some or all of the following traits may characterize the Christian who does not fully trust God:

disobedience	plagued by impure thoughts
lack of love for God and others	jealous
	worrisome
inconsistent prayer life	easily discouraged, frustrated
lack of desire for Bible study	critical
legalistic attitude	lack of purpose

Note: The individual who professes to be a Christian but who continues to practice sin should realize that he may not be a Christian at all, according to Ephesians 5:5 and 1 John 2:3; 3:6, 9.

Spirit-Centered Christians

When a Christian puts Christ on the throne of his life, he yields to God's control. This Christian's interests are directed by the Holy Spirit, resulting in harmony with God's plan.

- *"But the fruit of the Spirit is love, joy, peace, patience, kindness, goodness, faithfulness, gentleness and self-control. Against such things there is no law"* (Galatians 5:22-23).

Jesus said:

- *"I have come that they may have life, and have it to the full"* (John 10:10b).

- *"I am the vine; you are the branches. If a man remains in me and I in him, he will bear much fruit; apart from me you can do nothing"* (John 15:5).

- *"But you will receive power when the Holy Spirit comes on you; and you will be my witnesses in Jerusalem, and in all Judea and Samaria, and to the ends of the earth"* (Acts 1:8).

The following traits result naturally from the Holy Spirit's work in our lives:

Christ centered	love
Holy Spirit empowered	joy
motivated to tell others about Jesus	peace
	patience
dedicated to prayer	kindness
student of God's Word	goodness
trusts God	faithfulness
obeys God	gentleness
	self-control

The degree to which these traits appear in a Christian's life and marriage depends upon the extent to which the Christian trusts the Lord with every detail of life, and upon that person's maturity in Christ. One who is only beginning to understand the ministry of the Holy Spirit should not be discouraged if he is not as fruitful as mature Christians who have known and experienced this truth for a longer period of time.

Giving God Control

Jesus promises his followers an abundant and fruitful life as they allow themselves to be directed and empowered by the Holy Spirit. As we give God control of our lives, Christ lives in and through us in the power of the Holy Spirit (John 15).

If you sincerely desire to be directed and empowered by God, you can turn your life over to the control of the Holy Spirit right now (Matthew 5:6; John 7:37-39).

First, confess your sins to God, agreeing with him that you want to turn from any past sinful patterns in your life. Thank God in faith that he has forgiven all of your sins because Christ died for you (Colossians 2:13-15; 1 John 1:9; 2:1-3; Hebrews 10:1-18).

Be sure to offer every area of your life to God (Romans 12:1-2). Consider what areas you might rather keep to yourself, and be sure you're willing to give God control in those areas.

By faith, commit yourself to living according to the Holy Spirit's guidance and power.

- *Live by the Spirit:* **"So I say, live by the Spirit, and you will not gratify the desires of the sinful nature. For the sinful nature desires what is contrary to the Spirit, and the Spirit what is contrary to the sinful nature. They are in conflict with each other, so that you do not do what you want"** (Galatians 5:16-17).

- *Trust in God's promise:* **"This is the confidence we have in approaching God: that if we ask anything according to his will, he hears us. And if we know that he hears us—whatever we ask—we know that we have what we asked of him"** (1 John 5:14-15).

Expressing Your Faith Through Prayer

Prayer is one way of expressing your faith to God. If the prayer that follows expresses your sincere desire, consider praying the prayer or putting the thoughts into your own words:

> **Dear God, I need you. I acknowledge that I have been directing my own life and that, as a result, I have sinned against you. I thank you that you have forgiven my sins through Christ's death on the cross for me. I now invite Christ to take his place on the throne of my life. Take control of my life through the Holy Spirit as you promised you would if I asked in faith. I now thank you for directing my life and for empowering me through the Holy Spirit.**

Walking in the Spirit

If you become aware of an area of your life (an attitude or an action) that is displeasing to God, simply confess your sin, and thank God that he has forgiven your sins on the basis of Christ's death on the cross. Accept God's love and forgiveness by faith, and continue to have fellowship with him.

If you find that you've taken back control of your life through sin—a definite act of disobedience—try this exercise, "Spiritual Breathing," as you give that control back to God.

1. Exhale. Confess your sin. Agree with God that you've sinned against him, and thank him for his forgiveness of it, according to 1 John 1:9 and Hebrews 10:1-25. Remember that confession involves repentance, a determination to change attitudes and actions.

2. Inhale. Surrender control of your life to Christ, inviting the Holy Spirit to once again take charge. Trust that he now directs and empowers you, according to the command of Galatians 5:16-17 and the promise of 1 John 5:14-15. Returning to your faith in God enables you to continue to experience God's love and forgiveness.

Revolutionizing Your Marriage

This new commitment of your life to God will enrich your marriage. Sharing with your spouse what you've committed to is a powerful step in solidifying this commitment. As you exhibit the Holy Spirit's work within you, your spouse may be drawn to make the same commitment you've made. If both of you have given control of your lives to the Holy Spirit, you'll be able to help each other remain true to God, and your marriage may be revolutionized. With God in charge of your lives, life becomes an amazing adventure.

Leaders Notes

Contents

About Leading a HomeBuilders Group **131**

About the Leaders Notes **134**

Session One **135**

Session Two **141**

Session Three **145**

Session Four **150**

Session Five **154**

Session Six **157**

About Leading a HomeBuilders Group

What is the leader's job?

Your role is that of "facilitator"—one who encourages people to think and to discover what Scripture says, who helps group members feel comfortable, and who keeps things moving forward.

What is the best setting and time schedule for this study?

This study is designed as a small-group home Bible study. However, it can be adapted for use in a Sunday school setting as well. Here are some suggestions for using this study in a small group and in a Sunday school class:

In a small group

To create a friendly and comfortable atmosphere, it is recommended that you do this study in a home setting. In many cases, the couple that leads the study also serves as host to the group. Sometimes involving another couple as host is a good idea. Choose the option you believe will work best for your group, taking into account factors such as the number of couples participating and the location.

Each session is designed as a ninety-minute study, but we recommend a two-hour block of time. This will allow you to move through each part of the study at a more relaxed pace. However, be sure to keep in mind one of the cardinal rules of a small group: Good groups start *and* end on time. People's time is valuable, and your group will appreciate your being respectful of this.

In a Sunday school class

There are two important adaptations you need to make if you

want to use this study in a class setting: (1) The material you cover should focus on the content from the Blueprints section of each session. Blueprints is the heart of each session and is designed to last sixty minutes. (2) Most Sunday school classes are taught in a teacher format instead of a small-group format. If this study will be used in a class setting, the class should adapt to a small-group dynamic. This will involve an interactive, discussion-based format and may also require a class to break into multiple smaller groups (we recommend groups of six to eight people).

What is the best size group?

We recommend from four to eight couples (including you and your spouse). If you have more people interested than you think you can accommodate, consider asking someone else to lead a second group. If you have a large group, you are encouraged at various times in the study to break into smaller subgroups. This helps you cover the material in a timely fashion and allows for optimum interaction and participation within the group.

What about refreshments?

Many groups choose to serve refreshments, which help create an environment of fellowship. If you plan on including refreshments in your study, here are a couple of suggestions: (1) For the first session (or two) you should provide the refreshments and then allow the group to be involved by having people sign up to bring them on later dates. (2) Consider starting your group with a short time of informal fellowship and refreshments (fifteen minutes), then move into the study. If couples are late, they miss only the food and don't disrupt the study. You may also want to have refreshments available at the end of your meeting to encourage fellowship, but remember, respect the group members' time by ending the study on schedule and allowing anyone who needs to leave right away the opportunity to do so gracefully.

What about child care?

Groups handle this differently depending on their needs. Here are a couple of options you may want to consider:

- Have group members be responsible for making their own arrangements.
- As a group, hire child care, and have all the kids watched in one location.

What about prayer?

An important part of a small group is prayer. However, as the leader, you need to be sensitive to the level of comfort the people in your group have toward praying in front of others. Never call on people to pray aloud if you don't know if they are comfortable doing this. There are a number of creative approaches you can take, such as modeling prayer, calling for volunteers, and letting people state their prayers in the form of finishing a sentence. A tool that is helpful in a group is a prayer list. You are encouraged to utilize a prayer list, but let it be someone else's ministry to the group. You should lead the prayer time, but allow another couple in the group the opportunity to create, update, and distribute prayer lists.

In closing

An excellent resource that covers leading a HomeBuilders group in greater detail is the *HomeBuilders Leader Guide* by Drew and Kit Coons. This book may be obtained at your local Christian bookstore or by contacting Group Publishing or FamilyLife.

About the Leaders Notes

The sessions in this study can be easily led without a lot of preparation time. However, accompanying Leaders Notes have been provided to assist you in preparation. The categories within the Leaders Notes are as follows:

Objectives

The purpose of the Objectives is to help focus on the issues that will be presented in each session.

Notes and Tips

This section will relate any general comments about the session. This information should be viewed as ideas, helps, and suggestions. You may want to create a checklist of things you want to be sure to do in each session.

Commentary

Included in this section are notes that relate specifically to Blueprints questions. Not all Blueprints questions in each session will have accompanying commentary notes. Questions with related commentaries are designated by numbers (for example, Blueprints question 2 in Session One would correspond to number 2 in the Commentary section of Session One Leaders Notes).

Session One:
The Traps of Adolescence

Objectives

To pass biblical convictions to your teenage children that will equip them to avoid the traps of adolescence, you need to stay connected with them.

In this session, parents will...

- enjoy getting to know one another.
- examine some of the challenges of maintaining a close relationship with children as they enter the adolescent years.
- identify "traps" that can entice and lure teenagers into making foolish choices.
- reflect on their need to pass on biblical convictions to their children.

Notes and Tips

1. Welcome to the first session of the HomeBuilders course *Guiding Your Teenagers*. In this first session, the focus should be on relaxing and making sure that everyone feels as comfortable as possible. A sense of comfort in the group will allow individuals to more easily share serious issues later in the study.

As the leader, set a tone of openness by sharing on a personal level. The degree to which you are open and willing to share during this course will have a direct effect on the level of sharing that occurs in the group.

2. If you have not already done so, you will want to read the information on pages 4 and 5 as well as "About Leading a HomeBuilders Group" and "About the Leader's Notes" starting on page 131.

3. A great resource book for you—and to recommend to your group members—is *Parenting Today's Adolescent* by Dennis and Barbara Rainey. This book includes in-depth discussions of each of the traps of adolescence covered in this HomeBuilders study.

4. As part of the first session, review with the group the "Ground Rules" (see page 11 in the Introduction).

5. While it is anticipated that the majority of participants in your group will be couples, you may also have single parents or one parent from a marriage represented. Regardless of the mix of people who come, this course can be beneficial to all parents of teens and preteens. However, be aware that throughout this study you will find certain features that are specifically designed for couples, such as designated couples questions and the HomeBuilders Projects.

As the leader, be flexible and sensitive to your group. For example, if you do have a single parent in your group, invite him or her to join you and your spouse when a couples question is indicated. If you have multiple single parents, they may want to answer these questions together. Likewise, for the HomeBuilders Projects at the end of every session, encourage singles to complete what they can individually, or to work with another single parent on the project.

6. You will notice that there is a call-out note at the start of Blueprints that recommends breaking into smaller groups.

The reason for this is twofold: (1) to help facilitate discussion and participation by everyone, and (2) to help you be able to get through the material in the allotted time.

7. In this study you will find questions that are designed for spouses to answer together (like questions 11 and 12 in this session). The purpose of these "couples questions" is to foster communication and unity between spouses and to give couples an opportunity to deal with personal issues. While couples are free to share their responses to these questions with the group, be sensitive to the fact that not all couples will want to do so.

8. Because this is the first session, make a special point to tell the group about the importance of the HomeBuilders Projects, which they should try and complete in between group meetings. These projects help people apply the principles discussed in each session directly in their lives. Encourage couples to "Make a Date" before the next meeting to work on this session's project. Mention that you will ask about their experience with the project at the next session.

In addition to the HomeBuilders Projects, there are six Parent-Teen Interactions—one related to each session. These interactions (starting on page 104) are an invaluable opportunity for parents to communicate with their teenagers, and are designed to help parents pass on biblical convictions for the topics addressed in this course. Though we recommend that parents try to complete the interactions in between group sessions, we know that this will be a challenge. We encourage couples to place a priority on completing the HomeBuilders Projects, and then doing the Parent-Teen Interactions when they have time, whether in between sessions or at a later date.

9. Since this is the first session, you may want to offer a closing prayer instead of asking others to pray aloud. Many people are uncomfortable praying in front of others, and unless you already know your group well, it may be wise to slowly venture into various methods of prayer.

10. With this group just getting under way, it's not too late to invite others to join the group. During Wrap-Up, challenge everyone to think about someone he or she could invite to the next session.

Commentary

Here is some additional information about various Blueprints questions. The numbers that follow correspond to the Blueprints questions of the same numbers in the session. Be aware, notes are not included for every question. Many of the questions in this study are designed for group members to draw from their own opinions and experiences. If you share any of these points, be sure to do so in a manner that does not stifle discussion by making you the authority with the "real answers." As you share these notes, keep in mind that these sessions are designed around group interaction and participation.

2. Realize that there may be multiple, different solutions offered here. Be careful not to judge or criticize. The goal of this question is to spark interaction, not to seek agreement on one right approach or answer.

3. Most teenagers lack the maturity, basic life experience, and biblical convictions to make wise long-term decisions. By not grasping the lasting impact their decisions can have, and without the knowledge of certain consequences, teens can and often do make costly mistakes. They are influenced by

worldly philosophies they find in the media, and they are
often encouraged toward foolish and rebellious behavior by
their peers. As a result, they need our guidance.

4. Because of our sin nature, we all tend to act in foolish ways
that expose us to unnecessary dangers, both physical and
spiritual. The foolish person tends to reject the limits or
commands of God that have been given as an act of love and
protection. This applies to parents as well as children, but
teenagers are often placed in situations where this foolishness can have harsh consequences. For example:

- speeding in an automobile without thinking about the
  dangers involved
- experimenting with alcohol, drugs, or cigarettes because
  they think it won't hurt them to "just give it a try"
- taking a drink or eating something at a party without
  asking what it is
- hiding a mistake, a sin, or foolhardy act from parents

5. It's more difficult to build and maintain a relationship with
children as they enter adolescence. They begin to "pull
away" emotionally—they want to be with friends more, they
are more independent, and they don't want to spend as much
time with their parents. When this happens, some parents
pull away themselves and fail to put the same effort into
building and maintaining a relationship with their children.
In addition, some parents may feel awkward guiding their
children at this age because of mistakes they made at the
same age. Or they just plain give up, feeling there is little
more they can do to influence their children.

Note: The focus of the discussion for this question may tend
to focus only on the negative aspects of adolescents expressing greater independence from their parents. If this is a

concern, consider asking this question: In what ways is increasing independence a natural and healthy part of growing up?

6. Parents should fear God and keep God's commandments. In order to teach their children about God and the Bible, parents need to be involved in different aspects of their lives so they have the freedom to talk about how to walk with God in each of those situations. Discussions about God and the Bible should permeate the conversations parents have with their children.

9. God's Word provides guidance for practically every decision we make in our lives, and walking in the truth means ordering your everyday life around biblical convictions.

10. Some suggestions: praying with your teen about specific needs, reading the Bible or memorizing Scripture together, encouraging your teen to develop spiritually through a devotional life, attending worship together, and reading and discussing the biographies of outstanding Christians.

12. It is by living out biblical convictions—taking an unpopular stand, refusing to compromise in public settings, calling the family to prayer—that you can show your children that convictions based on the Word of God are more important than what people think or the consequences that may come. They will know that believing God and the Word of God is not only worth living for, but also worth dying for.

Attention HomeBuilders Leaders

FamilyLife invites you to register your HomeBuilders group. Your registration connects you to the HomeBuilders Leadership Network, a worldwide movement of couples who are using HomeBuilders to strengthen marriages and families in their communities. You'll receive the latest news about HomeBuilders and other ministry opportunities to help strengthen marriages and families in your community. As the HomeBuilders Leadership Network grows, we will offer additional resources such as online training, prayer requests, and chat with authors. There is no cost or obligation to register; simply go to www.familylife.com/homebuilders.

Session Two:
Peer Pressure

Objectives

Your involvement in your teenager's life will help your teen make wise choices in choosing friends and in resisting unhealthy influence from peers.

In this session, parents will...

- discuss the incredible influence peers have on adolescents.
- examine what the Bible says about the power of peer relationships.
- share thoughts on how to stay involved in their teens' lives.

Notes and Tips

1. If new people join the group this session, during Warm-Up ask them to share the names and ages of their children and why they came to this group. Also, give a brief summary of the main points from Session One, and have the group pass around their books to record contact information (page 14).

2. If you're planning on having refreshments, make sure the arrangements are covered.

3. If your group has decided to use a prayer list, make sure this is covered.

4. For this session's Warm-Up, you will need to set up a mini obstacle course. You'll need six to eight sheets of paper, a blindfold, and six to eight different "obstacles" (common, safe, nonbreakable household items, books, chairs, plastic containers—whatever you have handy).

If you choose to let multiple people experience the obstacle course, you may spend longer than fifteen minutes on the Warm-Up section. If this happens, try to still finish the Blueprints section in forty-five to sixty minutes. It's a good idea to mark the questions in Blueprints that you want to be sure to cover. Encourage group members to look at any questions you don't get to during the session when they do the HomeBuilders Project for this session.

5. If you told the group during the first session that you'd be asking them to relate something they learned from the first HomeBuilders Project, be sure to do so. The Project Report time can help establish an environment of mutual accountability. Be prepared to share a personal example of your own.

6. For the closing prayer in this session, you may want to ask for a volunteer or two to close the group in prayer. Check ahead of time with a couple of people you think might be comfortable praying aloud.

7. Looking ahead: For the Warm-Up in Session Three, you will need to have copies of several popular magazines. Ideally these would be publications that you and members of your group subscribe to or read on a regular basis. Before you end this session, you may want to ask group members to bring a magazine with them to the next meeting (it doesn't matter if it's current or old).

Commentary

3. Peers often ridicule the standards and values you teach at home, and they encourage deceit and rebellion. As a result, teenagers stop listening to their parents at the very time when they need their guidance more than ever.

Note: The numbers that follow correspond to the Blueprints questions of the same numbers in the session.

Some examples of ways peers undermine parental authority include making fun of parents' rules, ridiculing teens who try to obey their parents, tempting other teens to reject parental authority, and encouraging their friends to lie to their parents.

6. Spending time with those who exhibit attitudes or behaviors that are rebellious to God's Word can have a powerful influence on anyone—even teenagers with the best training at home. An outstanding teenager may be influenced negatively by constant exposure to teenagers involved in wrong activities. Sometimes the association with "bad company" can begin innocuously—notice the progression in Psalm 1:1-3 from walking with, to standing in the company of, and, finally, sitting with those who mock God.

7. Friends play a critical role in our spiritual maturity. Good friends can encourage you to walk closely with God.

9. A parent's role changes often by default. Parents may think that choosing friends happens naturally through common interests. While that is often true, there are also children who actively try to influence your teenager.

10. As we discussed in the previous session, teenagers will often make foolish choices. You must not give up the right to assist and determine who has the strongest influence on your teen.

11. We all need emotional connections to other people. A child who is distant from parents will eventually need to have emotional needs met. Peers will perform this role. This is one reason gangs are such a powerful influence on teenagers. They offer acceptance, relationships, and meaning to a drifting teen's life.

Session Three:
Sex

Objectives

You can help your teenagers avoid the trap of sex by challenging them to a high standard of purity and innocence.

In this session, parents will...

- examine their convictions relating to sexuality and their teenagers.
- reflect on the preparation they have given—or need to give—their children to face the trap of sex as a teen.
- look at what God's Word says about sex.
- consider the influence the culture at large has on how teens view sex.

Notes and Tips

1. By this session, group members have probably warmed up a bit to each other, but may not yet feel comfortable enough to open up and share on a deeper personal level. Don't force the issue. Continue to encourage everyone to attend and to complete their projects.

2. For this session's Warm-Up, you will need to have copies of several popular magazines (current or old—women's, news, sports, entertainment, and health magazines would all work well). Even better would be a selection of teen magazines. Pick up from the store, or borrow from teenagers, copies of popular teen magazines such as Seventeen, Teen People, YM, Cosmo Girl, and Thrasher.

And for the breakout groups this Warm-Up calls for, you may want to consider creating subgroups of the same gender. This will provide an opportunity to see what, if any, differences there may be between how men and women assess what they consider to be inappropriate content.

3. For Extra Impact: If you don't end up having copies of magazines for the Warm-Up, you could start the session in this way: Say, "We live in a culture that is permeated by sex. If you turn on the television and watch regular network shows, it won't take long for you to hear sexual jokes, innuendos, and other sexually suggestive references." Then ask these questions: "What philosophy do you think lies behind many of these messages? How do you think children are affected by these messages as they grow up?"

4. Question 6 in Blueprints calls for couples to look up different Scripture passages. This approach allows for the group to simultaneously examine multiple passages. This saves time and gives the group a chance to learn from one another.

5. During the Wrap-Up, continue to encourage couples to "Make a Date" to complete the HomeBuilders Projects between sessions. The serious subjects addressed in Sessions 3-6 cannot be covered in depth in the group session alone. The projects for these sessions will help group members be able to evaluate these important topics in a more personal and deeper way.

6. Congratulations! With the completion of this session, you will be halfway through this study. It's time for a leader checkup: How are you feeling? How is the group going? What has worked well so far? What things might you consider changing as you approach the remaining sessions?

Commentary

3. If we let our own past mistakes and sinful behavior prevent us from teaching our children the truth of God's Word, we would never feel free to teach them about anything.

Note: The numbers that follow correspond to the Blueprints questions of the same numbers in the session.

4. If not properly taught, your children will learn about this vital aspect of life from peers or the world. They will adopt the convictions of their peers or the world. Their curiosity will drive them to find answers.

Experimenting with the powerful emotional, physical, and spiritual bonding that occurs during sexual intimacy is like allowing children to play with matches and dynamite. Of course, in addition to the emotional scarring and guilt, there exists the danger of sickness or even death because of sexually transmitted diseases.

6. *Genesis 1:27-28:* Sex is for procreation in marriage.
Genesis 2:22-25: God created sex.
Proverbs 5:18-19: Sex is for intimacy and pleasure in marriage.
1 Corinthians 7:2-4: Sex is to be enjoyed by a man and woman in marriage.
Hebrews 13:4: Sex outside marriage is sin.

7. God wants the best for us. Here are a few benefits of remaining pure until marriage:
- By waiting you please God.
- By waiting you build trust, which is necessary for intimacy.
- By waiting you develop the God-honoring qualities of patience and self-control.
- By waiting you affirm that you care more for the other person than for yourself.

- By waiting you protect yourself from feelings of guilt and shame.
- By waiting you provide yourself with an example to give your children.
- By waiting you are protected from emotional, mental, and physical trauma should you break off your relationship.
- By waiting you develop healthy communication habits and skills.
- By waiting you avoid the possibility of an unwanted pregnancy.
- By waiting you maintain a clear conscience before God and man.
- By waiting you increase the anticipation and enjoyment of your wedding night.
- By waiting you experience the blessing of obedience.
- By waiting you discover more about each other than just the physical.
- By waiting you maintain a witness to a lost world.
- By waiting you keep from bringing reproach on the name of Christ.

8. Suggested follow-up question: In what ways, if any, do you think responses would differ between Christian and non-Christian parents?

9. This is a growing view among teens; in recent years there has been an upswing of teens who engage in oral sex but don't think it is sex because it doesn't involve sexual intercourse. This type of "technical virginity" still violates God's commands against sexual immorality. It is also dangerous because there are diseases that are transmitted without sexual intercourse.

10. When it comes to sex, the Bible gives us a higher goal to set for our children than virginity. The goal of our instruction with our children should be to help protect their purity and innocence. These two God-given gifts are lost long before intercourse if your teen begins to experience the sexual response that God designed for marriage. We must set our sights high and challenge our teenagers to the highest standard, God's standard. As parents, we should want our children to arrive at marriage innocent of evil, pure in their sexuality, and with a healthy view of marriage—not encumbered by a lot of emotional baggage from past sexual mistakes.

11. Keeping your children "innocent about what is evil" means trying to keep them from experiencing evil as much as you can. In today's culture, absolute innocence is impossible, of course. But it is possible to limit the amount of exposure and experience a child has.

Protecting the innocence of children involves at least three things. First, you must model purity in your own behavior. Second, you must set clear standards for your children in the area of sexual morality. Third, you must challenge your children to these standards and continue to stay in touch with them to see how they are holding to them. This can mean some uncomfortable conversations and questions such as "Where are you drawing the line when you go out on a date?"

Session Four:
Dating

Objectives

One of the greatest challenges for parents is to set solid standards for their teens as they begin dating.

In this session, parents will...

- discuss the nature and practice of dating in today's culture.
- reflect on their responsibility to set standards for their teens.
- look at and discuss Scriptures related to the key issues surrounding dating.

Notes and Tips

1. As the leader of a HomeBuilders group, one of the best things you can do is to pray specifically for each group member. Take time to pray as you prepare for this session.

2. Remember the importance of starting and ending on time.

3. By this time group members should be getting more comfortable with one another. For prayer time at the end of this session, you may want to give everyone an opportunity to pray by asking people to finish a sentence like "Lord, I want to thank you for..." Be sensitive to anyone who may not feel comfortable doing this.

4. You may find it helpful to make some notes right after the meeting to help you evaluate how this session went. Ask yourself questions such as "Did everyone participate?" and "Is there anyone I need to make a special effort to follow up with before the next session?"

Commentary

1. Some of the reasons the dating game, as currently played by most people, can be a dangerous trap for teenagers are:

Note: The numbers that follow correspond to the Blueprints questions of the same numbers in the session.

- One-on-one dating leads couples to spend too much time alone at the peak of the sex drive for a young man.
- Teens make poor choices about who to date and are negatively influenced by those who do not share their values.
- Teens develop premature emotional attachments with the opposite sex.
- These emotional attachments cause them to desire a physical relationship of the same intensity.
- Acting either from peer pressure or from a need that is not met at home, teens begin pairing off as boyfriend and girlfriend when they are too young and immature to make good decisions.

2. Our popular media depicts a type of "fantasy love" where young people look to fulfill their romantic dreams and fantasies—and think nothing of dropping one relationship to pursue that fantasy with another person. It portrays an unbiblical view of sex—physical intimacy between unmarried couples is shown so continually that it is easy for teenagers to assume it should be a normal part of a dating relationship. It also encourages people to view marriage entirely within the context of personal fulfillment rather than unconditional commitment.

3. If a young person spends too much time in the emotionally and physically volatile environment of a relationship with the opposite sex, personal growth will be affected. Most of the time a teenager is not able to understand how emotional attachments form and that they usually lead to some type of physical expression. Early attachments serve no real positive purpose in a culture where most people do not select a spouse and marry until their twenties. Too much emphasis on early pairing off also robs children of other necessary and rewarding opportunities to develop their interests and social skills. It leaves them vulnerable to succumbing to sexual temptation at an early age. And, finally, the pattern of some of moving from one boyfriend or girlfriend to another may lay the groundwork for a restlessness and discontentment later in marriage.

4. Children need to learn the differences between men and women, and how to communicate with the opposite sex, treat the opposite sex with respect, handle conflict, understand and live out their roles as male and female, abide by their boundaries regarding sex, exercise control in the face of temptation, handle infatuation, develop friendships without forming unhealthy emotional attachments, interact with people of different personalities and temperaments, evaluate another person's character, determine the type of person to marry, discern God's will as they look for a spouse, and much more.

5. Key convictions or character qualities include learning how to treat the opposite sex with honor; avoid compromising situations; maintain physical, emotional, and spiritual purity; and be accountable to parents.

8. Your children may become prematurely independent—before they are ready to make life-affecting decisions for themselves. They need your guidance as they struggle with their convictions.

10. This passage is often cited as part of the answer to the question why a Christian shouldn't marry a non-Christian. But teenagers also should understand why it's not a good idea to seek any kind of romantic relationship with "unbelievers." If a teen falls into a relationship with an unbeliever, he or she runs a great risk of sliding away from a close relationship with God. Parents should help their teenagers evaluate their dating relationships. Not every person who uses the label "Christian" is sincere about his or her faith and seeking to grow in Christ. A teenager caught up in emotions may not be able to exercise this level of discernment about another person without a parent's loving, gentle assistance.

12. Related to this question, you may also want to look at Ephesians 6:2-3.

Children should honor both sets of parents by obeying them and encouraging their dates to do the same. They should show common courtesies. They should be willing to meet and talk with parents rather than avoiding them. Likewise, parental expectations, such as when a date is expected home, should be clarified and respected.

Session Five:
Media

Objectives

Teenagers need to develop discernment about the type and amount of media they consume.

In this session, parents will...

- think about and discuss the way media impacts family life.
- evaluate media on both a time and content basis.
- consider media standards from the perspective of a biblical basis.

Notes and Tips

1. You and your spouse may want to consider writing notes of thanks and encouragement to the members of your group this week. Thank them for their commitment and contribution to the group, and let them know that you are praying for them. (Make a point to pray for them as you write their notes.)

2. In this session, be prepared for differences in opinion on the quality and influence of various types of television shows, music, movies, and so forth. You may find that some group members have few standards about media, while others are very strict. Encourage the group to interact without an attitude of judgment. The greatest value of this type of discussion may be in how it challenges us as parents to evaluate the impact of media and set standards.

3. Looking ahead: For the next session—the last session of this study—you may want to have someone, or a couple, share what this study or group has meant to him or her. If you want to do this, think about who you will ask to share.

Commentary

1. One of the biggest problems with media—especially television—is that people let it take up too much of their time. In families it can prevent deep relationships from being built. Passive media consumption also can lead to an unhealthy desire to be entertained. You could say our entire culture is overly obsessed with entertainment.

Note: The numbers that follow correspond to the Blueprints questions of the same numbers in the session.

3. The tendency in this session may be to focus on the negative aspects of mass and popular media. In light of this, you may want to challenge the group to think about ways media—different forms and types—can be used in a positive way to improve the relationships they have with their teens.

4. Many adolescents have not learned how to make good choices about media, and lack discernment about good and bad messages. Many take their cues on how to dress and cut their hair, what to eat and drink, what music to listen to, what people to look up to, and so much more, from the media. The media messages our preteens and teenagers allow to enter their ears and eyes will sink deep into their minds and will affect their attitudes and behavior.

5. Ask people to give specific examples of what they've seen or heard in current movies, TV shows, or songs.

6. Often media will encourage us to do or believe things contrary to God's Word. Media influence things such as the importance we place upon material possessions, how we relate to other people, what we believe about the purpose and place of sexual intimacy, and more. Popular media often ridicules biblical morality, and feeds our selfish nature.

9. One approach to this question is to ask what kinds of things are true, noble, right, pure, lovely, admirable, excellent, or praiseworthy. Then ask, how can we focus on these good things while partaking of all the media choices that we are offered?

Session Six:
Substance Abuse

Objectives

Your connectedness with your teen, your integrity, and your walk with God will help your child deal with one of the deadliest traps of adolescence.

In this session, parents will...

* consider the consequences that teens and their families face from substance abuse.
* discuss selected passages of Scripture as they relate to substance abuse.
* close this course by discussing the need for them and their children to have a strong personal relationship with God.

Notes and Tips

1. Some group members may be threatened by this session's topic because of past experiences they have not shared with others, so be sensitive to those who seem hesitant to talk.

2. Blueprints question 10 in this session gives people in the group an opportunity to share about their personal relationship with God. You may want to consider asking ahead of time a couple of people in the group who you know would be comfortable answering this question to be prepared to briefly share what God has done in their lives.

3. While this HomeBuilders study has great value, people are likely to return to previous patterns of living unless they commit to a plan for carrying on the progress made. During this final session, encourage couples to take specific steps beyond this study. For example, you may want to challenge couples who have developed the habit of a "date night" to continue this practice. You may also want to discuss doing another HomeBuilders study.

4. **For Extra Impact:** A suggestion for making the closing prayer time of this last session special: Have the group form a prayer circle. Then have each couple or person, if comfortable doing so, take a turn standing or kneeling in the middle of the circle with the group praying specifically for that couple or person.

5. As a part of this last session, devote some time for planning one more meeting—a party to celebrate the completion of this study!

Commentary

Note: The numbers that follow correspond to the Blueprints questions of the same numbers in the session.

2. Reasons for experimentation include influence of TV and movies, rebellion, stress, curiosity, inability to stand up to peer pressure, desire to experiment with "grown-up" behaviors, a cry for help, and escape from reality.

3. These substances are damaging to the body: They can damage the brain, they can cause addiction and death, they can lead to other more dangerous life choices, and they often destroy family relationships.

First Corinthians 6:19-20 tells us that our bodies are not our own. As a Christian, the Holy Spirit dwells in you. When Jesus died on the cross, God purchased you from the control and destruction of sin. The battle within us is to yield to the

Spirit so we do not give our bodies over to destructive things.

7. Our model as parents is the first source of behavior and conviction our children have. Without a firm foundation in a relationship with us, it will be much more difficult for our teens to take a stand when facing temptations from peers or a larger group.

10. If you sense that not everyone in the group understands what it means to have a relationship with Christ, recommend for further reading the article "Our Problems, God's Answers" that starts on page 120.

11. There will be temptations and ideas presented to your teens that they cannot resist without the power and presence of God in their lives. In the final analysis, a relationship with Jesus Christ is the only reason to remain pure and undefiled by harmful substances.

12. Some truths that can be gleaned from this passage: Be obedient. Faithfully keep the commands of God, and teach them to your children. Don't be like those who have rejected God's commands. Avoid stubbornness and rebelliousness toward God. Be a loyal follower of God.

Does Your Church Offer Marriage Insurance?

Great marriages don't just happen—husbands and wives need to nurture them. They need to make their marriage relationship a priority.

That's where the HomeBuilders Couples Series® can help! The series consists of interactive 6- to 7-week small group studies that make it easy for couples to really open up with each other. The result is fun, non-threatening interactions that build stronger Christ-centered relationships between spouses—and with other couples!

Whether you've been married for years or are newly married, this series will help you and your spouse discover timeless principles from God's Word that you can apply to your marriage and make it the best it can be!

The HomeBuilders Leader Guide gives you all the information and encouragement you need to start and lead a dynamic HomeBuilders small group.

The HomeBuilders Couples Series includes these life-changing studies:

- Building Teamwork in Your Marriage
- Building Your Marriage (also available in Spanish!)
- Building Your Mate's Self-Esteem
- Growing Together in Christ
- Improving Communication in Your Marriage (also available in Spanish!)
- Making Your Remarriage Last
- Mastering Money in Your Marriage
- Overcoming Stress in Your Marriage
- Resolving Conflict in Your Marriage

And check out the HomeBuilders Parenting Series!

- Building Character in Your Children
- Establishing Effective Discipline for Your Children
- Guiding Your Teenagers
- Helping Your Children Know God
- Improving Your Parenting
- Raising Children of Faith

Look for the **HomeBuilders Couples Series and HomeBuilders Parenting Series** at your favorite Christian supplier or write:

P.O. Box 485, Loveland, CO 80539-0485.
www.grouppublishing.com